Home In
One Piece

by

John Wayne Thompson as told to Paula Crain Grosinger, RN

HOME IN ONE PIECE

Author - John Wayne Thompson
Writer - Paula Crain Grosinger
Publisher - McCleery & Sons Publishing
Editor in Chief - Steve Tweed

International Standard Book Number: 0-9712027-1-0
Printed in the United States of America

ACKNOWLEDGMENTS

WE WOULD LIKE TO THANK

Photographer Taro Yamasaki

North Dakota REC/RTC Magazine

Swedlund Photography

United Blood Services

North Memorial Medical Center
3303 North Oakdale
Robbinsdale, MN 55422

Victoria Principal

Front cover photo courtesy of Mutual of Omaha.
Back cover photo by Taro Yamasaki (1992).

Every effort has been made by the authors and publisher to give credit for photographs and materials contributed to the production of this book. We apologize for any errors or omissions. Please notify the publisher if we have wrongly attributed materials or photos.

FOREWORD

As editors and publishers, we are proud and delighted to meet talented North Dakotans whose words flow into wonderful new books. Our work has evolved into a privilege.

Never have we seen a more compelling or courageous story than *"Home in One Piece,"* by John Thompson and Paula Grosinger. Written with gripping detail, and peppered with John's unfailing wit, this is a book we believe will be remembered as an American classic in non-fiction. John Thompson has encountered celebrity, tragedy and triumph on a scale few would dare imagine, let alone experience. His honesty and simple bravery come through in the written word, and in sharing these qualities, he gives us all a lasting and generous gift. We can learn better how to defeat life's toughest opponent – despair – by reading this magnificent account.

John Thompson and Paula Grosinger have made this book a great read, with a brilliant, serene light glowing over every paragraph, through sad moments as well as happy ones.

Moreover, *"Home in One Piece"* is a truthful journey, both entertaining and insightful. I defy anyone to start this book and put it down unfinished. Its themes of survival, recovery and enduring hope underlie a stream of factual events so fast-paced and harrowing that the reader is soon mesmerized. We at McCleery and Sons believe that producing such an invaluable statement of human dignity is what publishing should be all about.

Steve Tweed
Senior Editor

To my parents, Larry and Karen Thompson.
Your love and courage pulled me through.

And to Tuffy, my hero.

In 1992, I lost both of my arms in a farm accident. After my accident, there were so many reports of my survival and recovery, that the media said my story had risen to the level of an "urban legend."

The "urban legend" description might be accurate. While watching a recent episode of a popular Sunday night cartoon on television, one of the characters said, "If that poor farm boy whose arms were ripped off by a thresher, could dial 911 with his nose, then I think I can take care of that baby." The details of my accident were slightly different than the description in the cartoon, but it was unmistakably a reference to me.

Personally, I found the attention I received following my accident baffling. Numerous accounts of my survival referred to my actions as "heroic." To my way of thinking, a hero is someone who does something for others. I simply reacted to my instincts for self-preservation.

It was my dog, my best friend, who was the true hero when I was injured. Ironically, the death of my dog was one of the most devastating things that happened after my accident. It put a fine point on my sense of loss, and magnified the stress I experienced as a side effect of unexpected celebrity.

I'm far from perfect and I don't try to be for the sake of others. So, if I offend anyone by what I have written, please be aware that the offense is unintentional.

There have been some very dark times since my accident. The course of my life was altered for better in some ways, for worse in others. After all, I was only eighteen and I had lived a rather sheltered life up to the time of my accident. I still had some growing up to do, which wasn't made easier by having to bear the "hero" label.

My family has also been deeply affected by the aftermath of

my accident. There were many times when my mother said she wished she had the "old John" back. At the same time, it's hard for me to believe I ever was that "old John." In many ways, I feel that person died in the accident.

It has not been easy to find contentment with who I am. When you're thrust into the international spotlight, you have to learn to deal with a lot of external expectations. I think my sense of humor is one of the reasons I've lived to tell this story, and the support of friends and family has made a difference. I've also learned that feeling good about myself is more important than what other people think.

I am finally comfortable with the person I've become, and the reaction to this story is unlikely to alter that self-perception. It still bothers me when people refer to me as a hero and have expectations about the way I should act. I'm just someone who's trying to find his own way. I think there are many examples of true heroes in the world. I'm not one of them.

My writer and I received a lot of advice, most of it well-intentioned, on how to present my story. It was suggested that we should fictionalize the account to make it more exciting. It was also suggested that we should include more romance or trauma in our version of events. We were told by some experts that the story of a farm boy who loses both arms in an accident, saves himself, and then has an operation to replant the arms wouldn't be interesting enough to appeal to today's reading audience.

I'm not very good at following advice when it goes against my internal compass. It was important to me to tell my story honestly. It was also important to find a writer who could put my words on paper in a way that represented my own voice. After reading my account, I hope you'll understand that I was just an ordinary person, a North Dakota farm kid to be exact, to whom something extraordinary happened. I want people to know that the accident is not who I am.

Finally, I believe each individual has within themselves extraordinary strength and power to overcome adversity. My hope is that each of you will be inspired to find that wellspring of power within yourselves and use it in the way that brings you the most happiness and fulfillment, regardless of what anyone else thinks.

Chapter I
January 11, 1992

That morning remains frozen in my memory, the events lingering expectantly like breath lingers in frigid winter air.

January on the northern plains has a unique crispness. Temperatures fall to double digits below zero and stay there for days. Sounds seem to travel farther, perhaps because there is a lack of living vegetation to absorb them, and the air appears clearer than at other times of the year.

Some people have the misconception that farmers don't work during the winter months. If that were true, North Dakota farmers would get five months of vacation every year. Winter weather usually sets in by early November and spring doesn't really arrive until mid April, but it's no vacation.

I was used to working in the cold. If you raise livestock, like my family did, you have to make sure the animals are well fed because they burn a lot of calories just maintaining their body temperature in the arctic cold. A hard winter takes its toll on the animals making it difficult for them to gain weight. Keeping equipment working is a challenge, too. You can bet that if something is going to break down, it will happen on one of the coldest days of the year. It's not unusual for metal parts to become so brittle that they shatter. The weather can also make the oil or diesel fuel in engines turn to a custard-like consistency.

When I worked outside in this kind of weather, I tried not to notice the wind chill was hanging in the frostbite range. I moved a little faster, but on the farm we always seemed to be moving fast just to keep up. We worked hard and steady, and sometimes we thought about the danger involved. But like most farmers, danger wasn't a consideration until it was too late.

It was the same that morning. There wasn't much snow on the ground, but it was cold. I was alone on the farm except for the livestock and our family dogs.

My parents had taken off for Bismarck, North Dakota's state capital, a drive of about 80 miles. A cousin of my mother's, Michelle Barkow, had been seriously injured in an automobile accident and was in the intensive care unit at one of the Bismarck hospitals. My mother was very concerned about Michelle's mother and had packed food to take for the family.

I stayed behind to take care of the chores, which included grinding barley to be used as feed for the livestock. Dressed in my jeans, t-shirt and a heavy insulated flannel shirt, I left the house with Tuffy, my Blue Heeler dog and my constant companion, following close behind.

Grinding feed was a job I'd done hundreds of times. Tuffy and I jogged the 100 yards from the house to where the grain truck was parked. Then I backed the truck into position to transfer the barley into the grinder.

The transfer of the grain is accomplished with an auger, a piece of equipment I'd also had lots of experience operating. It's a common piece of machinery that looks like a giant corkscrew. The auger is driven by the flywheel on a tractor using a power take-off or PTO shaft. The PTO is connected to the spindle on the rear of the tractor. The spindle rotates powering the PTO shaft. The power take-off in turn spins, sometimes over 5,000 times a minute, or at a rate of nearly 100 times per second. That's a surface speed of four feet per second. That rotation is ultimately transmitted to the auger.

If something gets too close to the PTO, it takes only an instant for it to become tightly wrapped. The machinery is unforgiving, and pulling free is impossible. Power take-offs are supposed to have shields to cover the moving parts so accidents are less likely to occur, but our PTO was old. The shield had broken off long ago and like many farmers we hadn't spent the fifty dollars it would have taken to replace it. There were always other expenses that seemed more important or necessary.

I don't know exactly how it happened. I think I stepped backwards off the grain wagon, and without realizing it moved too close to the machinery. Perhaps I slipped on a patch of ice. Regardless, my insulated shirt became caught in the power take-off and before I realized it, I was spinning. In an instant my whole body was whirling around the shaft. Suddenly I was flung to the ground and I was knocked unconscious.

That should have been the end of my story. I shouldn't have regained consciousness. If not for Tuffy, I would have drifted into irreversible shock while bleeding out onto the ground.

I don't know how long I was lying there. The machinery had thrown me face down onto the dirt. I awakened to Tuffy licking the side of my face. I opened my eyes and he stopped. He stood there looking at me with his head cocked to one side and his ears pointing straight up. His tail was wagging impatiently. The expression on his face made it seem as though he was saying, "What are you waiting for? You've got to get up buddy." It was a mixed look of urgency and encouragement.

I still didn't know what had happened to me. My t-shirt and insulated jacket were gone, and I felt strange. I certainly didn't know how dire my situation was. I wasn't in any pain. I didn't feel cold. In fact, I mainly felt numb.

I looked toward my right arm. The best way to describe how it felt was "weird."

"Strange that I can't see it," I thought.

I figured it was broken at some odd angle and was just stuck behind my back. It didn't "feel" like it was missing.

"No need to panic yet," I told myself.

At the same time I was looking toward my right arm, I was trying to push myself up with my left arm, but I wasn't moving. When I looked toward the left arm, I noticed it was missing above the elbow. Then, looking back again toward my right arm, it appeared that it was missing at the shoulder. I hadn't been able to tell at first because some of the skin had separated from the arm and was hanging from the shoulder along with my ulnar nerve. It gave me the sensation that my arm was still there.

I knew immediately that my situation was grave. The muscles tightened in my throat and stomach with the realization that my arms were gone, but I didn't take the time to worry about it.

If I had stopped to think about my predicament, I might not have been able to get off the ground. Instead, I decided to get up. First, I maneuvered onto my back by scissoring my legs. Then, using my legs, I pushed myself backward inching close to one of the large rear tractor tires. I got my back against the tire and hoisted myself up with my legs. Once I was standing, I took another look at myself and the impact of what had just occurred finally hit me. Then I panicked.

I started screaming.

"Look at me! My God, look at me!"

Of course, there was no one within miles who could hear me. Tuffy and I stood there alone in the cold. I realized I had to stay calm.

"Okay," I told myself. "You're still alive and you're standing. This isn't your time to go."

I looked at Tuffy, who was standing right beside me.

"What are you standing there for?" he seemed to ask.

"You're right. We're going to the house, Tuffy. Ready?"

I started to walk the four hundred feet to the house. Tuffy was with me, staying beside me as if to say, "Keep going John. You can make it. I'm right here with you."

I was moving rather quickly, lurching and stumbling actually, and trying to maintain my balance. The movement made the nerve dangling from my right shoulder swing back and forth. Since my shirt and jacket had been ripped off in the accident, the nerve eventually hit me on my bare chest. It stuck there because it was covered with blood which froze to my skin.

I don't know how long the walk actually took me. It seemed like seconds, even if it was the longest walk of my life. The closer I got to the house the more I accelerated my pace. As long as I was moving under my own steam, I didn't want to lose momentum.

I made it to our back deck hoping I would be able to push the sliding glass door open with the bone that was sticking out of my left shoulder. When I put my shoulder to the door and started to push, the bone just bent back because it was broken. All the muscles that held it in position had been ripped away, too. The door was usually locked anyway, so I didn't waste time trying to slide it open with my feet.

After making it this far, I wasn't going to give up. The next thing to try was the door which led from the garage into the kitchen. To get at it, I first had to get in the garage. Luckily, the back door into the garage was open, so I was able to walk in. When I entered the garage I noticed Tuffy also came in, and he never came in the garage. He wouldn't leave my side until I was safely inside the house.

I got to the door leading into the house but the screen door was shut. I was wearing cowboy boots and I was able to get the toe of my boot between the screen door and the door frame and wedge it open. After getting the screen door open, I pushed on the inner door. It was shut tight. I had to get it open and quickly. Without thinking I dropped to my knees and bit the doorknob with my mouth.

Thankfully, it wasn't as cold in the garage as it was outside. My mouth might have frozen to the doorknob and then I would have been in a real fix. I turned my head, the knob twisted, and the door swung open.

The nearest phone was in our dining area but it was an old rotary dial model. I knew I had to get to the office because it had a push button phone. Standing in the kitchen doorway I looked down and noticed that the throw rug I was standing on was soaked with blood. To get to the office I would have to cross the new carpet my mother had just purchased for the dining room.

"If I can just keep this throw rug under me, I won't get the new carpet bloody," I said to myself.

I soon realized the futility of trying to spare the new carpet and gave up on using the throw rug as a shield. I walked quickly to the office only to find that door was also shut.

This latest frustration was almost too much. I started hitting the office door with my knee without much success. I put a knee-sized hole in the door, but that was it. I didn't dare kick it because I was afraid I'd lose my balance. Finally, I squatted down, bit the knob as I had with the outside door, and was able to get in.

I moved to the desk and knocked the receiver off the phone with my nose. I tried calling my friend Lee Anne by pushing the numbers with my nose. It took a lot of tries, but when I finally got the number right the line was busy. I didn't have time to get frustrated so I disconnected and tried to call my 17-year-old cousin Tammy who lived three and half miles away.

It didn't occur to me to call the ambulance myself even though I had the phone number memorized. This was before the time of enhanced 911 emergency response systems in our area. You still had to know the emergency service providers' numbers and dial them in full if you needed help.

I made a few failed attempts at punching Tammy's number with my nose before I decided to take a pen in my teeth. Finally, I got the number right. The phone rang a couple of times and Tammy picked up. I took a deep breath. Then, trying to stay calm, I leaned over the desk and spoke into the receiver.

"I lost both of my arms and you need to call the ambulance," I said.

"Who is this?" Tammy asked.

She sounded like she thought it was a prank phone call. Even though I was trying to sound calm, I'm sure I was speaking so rapidly that she had difficulty making sense of what I said.

"It's me — John!" I said.

She didn't understand me the first time I identified myself, so I repeated the words.

"It's me, John," I repeated. "I lost both my arms and I need an ambulance!"

Either the impact of what I'd said hadn't registered, or she thought I was kidding around. I admit, I'd earned a reputation as a practical joker, but it didn't take her long to come to the conclusion this was serious. It really was a full-fledged emergency.

I thought Tammy said she was going to call the ambulance. I

struggled to hang up the phone thinking she wouldn't be able to make another call unless I broke the connection. Tammy remembers it a little bit differently. She says the line went dead as soon as I told her it was me.

The blood flow was still heavy. By now the carpet, desk and office chair were covered. I didn't want any more blood to soak into the carpets so I walked across the hall to the bathroom. I stepped into the bathtub and squatted down on my heels, leaning against the side wall of the tub with the shower curtain shut.

Looking at myself again, I began to realize how desperate the situation was.

"This is terrible," I thought. "What's my mother going to do if she comes home and finds I died like this? I can't die."

I was covered in blood and wanted to get cleaned up before anyone saw me. It's one of those personal quirks, but I've always been picky about the way I look. I wanted to take a shower before anyone got there, but I figured it would probably be painful. Besides, I couldn't get undressed — so I just sat there and waited while our other dog Tinker stood barking outside the tub.

Tinker, a miniature poodle, was our house pet. I'm sure Tuffy, obedient about not coming into the house, never left the garage. He likely spent the entire time outside the kitchen door waiting for something to happen.

It didn't take long before I heard a car drive into the yard and someone come in the house. Then I heard my Aunt Renee, call for me.

"I'm in here," I called back to her from behind the shower curtain.

After Tammy called for the ambulance, she called her mom Renee at work. Renee raced to their house, which was on the way to our farm. She picked Tammy up and then hurried on to our place.

Neither Tammy or Renee knew what to expect, but following the blood trail to the bathroom door, Renee knew it was bad.

"I need to take a look at you, John."

"It's really bad, Aunt Renee. You won't want to see this. It's too awful."

I didn't want Renee to see me in that horrific state. It would probably give her nightmares for years to come. I insisted Tammy wasn't going to see me either, so she didn't come into the bathroom. But Renee stood outside the bathtub.

"I've got to take a look," Renee said patiently from the opposite side of the shower curtain. "Maybe I can help."

By this time, the blood flow had eased. Perhaps the worst was over, so I relented and let Renee pull the shower curtain back. She got an eye full. Looking at her expression, I wondered for a moment if I hadn't made a mistake in letting her see me. Her eyes got big, and she drew in a deep breath.

Then she told me it would be all right.

"They can put your arms back on," she said trying to sound like it was a known fact. I knew she was trying to stay calm, and reassure me at the same time, but her facial expression didn't match her voice.

My back felt like it was on fire.

"Do I still have any skin left on my back?" I asked.

"There's a nice scratch," Renee answered after taking a look, "but it's nothing to worry about."

She sat down on the seat of the toilet stool across from the tub, and we started talking about what had happened. I told her how Tuffy had licked my face to wake me up.

"If it hadn't been for him, I'd still be lying on the ground out there."

"How did you get up and get to the house?" she asked.

"I used my legs to push myself up against the tractor tire. Once I was standing, I just walked up to the house as fast as I could."

"Well, how on earth did you get inside?" she asked.

"I tried the sliding glass door first, but that didn't work," I explained. "Then I went into the garage. I used my mouth to open the side door into the kitchen."

Renee looked incredulous.

"I've heard of people having great strength in an emergency because of an adrenaline rush, but that's unbelievable," she said.

Trying to relieve the pressure of the situation, I started telling jokes.

Renee told me it was a good sign that my sense of humor was still intact.

By now, the blood flow was minimal but I was starting to feel weak and shaky. I also had an overwhelming sense of thirst.

"I feel like I'm dying of thirst," I told Renee. My use of the word dying struck me as ironic.

"Farm boy loses arms, but dies of thirst," I joked. "What a headline. Renee, do you think I could I have a drink of water?"

Renee poured me a glass and helped me drink it down. She told me I couldn't stay sitting the way I was. I felt like I was spinning, and I was incredibly tired. As much as I wanted to go to sleep, I knew I had to stay awake if I was going to survive.

Renee helped me step out of the bathtub and to the seat of the toilet stool. She held me up and told me to keep talking to her. I told some more jokes, but I knew I was dangerously close to shock or even death from the bleeding. I didn't want to dwell on dying, so I just kept talking and telling jokes.

"How many Montanans does it take to screw in a light bulb?..."

It seemed as though it was taking forever for the ambulance to get there.

"Where are they?" I complained to Renee.

"They'll be here in a few seconds," she said.

So I counted.

"One thousand one, one thousand two, one thousand three... Why is it taking so long?"

"Just a few more minutes."

I'd count some more and ask about the ambulance again. After a while I started to think about what it would be like for my parents when they got home.

"I'm so sorry about mom's new carpet."

"Your mom isn't going to care about the carpet," Renee said.

"But she works so hard, and now it will have to be replaced. It's going to cost a lot of money."

"Don't worry about the carpet."

"I bet dad is going to blame himself for leaving me here alone." '

We sat in the bathroom waiting and talking like that for about twenty minutes. The ambulance crew was dispatched from the town of Bowdon, a distance of about 15 miles to our farm. They thought they were responding to an accident involving a broken arm. I certainly had a surprise in store for them.

When the ambulance finally arrived, it brought three emergency medical technicians. Londa Neumiller and Joan Rodacker were veteran emergency medical technicians. Rick Flatten, who was also the Bowdon Elevator manager, was new. He had just completed his training two days before and this was his inaugural run. Like most rural ambulance squads, they were all volunteers who had to leave their homes or jobs when they received an emergency call.

Once inside our house they quickly figured out they were dealing with something more serious than a broken arm. There was more blood than any of them had ever seen before. However, they were still completely surprised when they entered the bathroom and saw Renee holding me.

"John's got no arms," Renee told them.

They filed into the bathroom in a row, got a quick look at me, and turned around and filed out in a row. I knew these people, and I knew shock when I saw it on their faces. My dad did business with Rick at the elevator. Londa was a school bus driver, and I went to school with one of Joan's children. I knew it was hard on them to see me in that condition.

All three were overwhelmed by the severity of my injuries, but needed only a few seconds to collect themselves so they could deal with the situation. Rick and Joan started asking where my arms were.

"I was working down at the grain bin by the tractor," I explained. "You should try to turn the tractor off because I think it's still running."

I was concerned because I didn't want the auger to run empty. It could ruin the equipment, and that would be another big expense. While

I was waiting alone in the bathtub, I had considered shutting the tractor down before anyone got there, but I couldn't figure out any way I could do it.

Rick took off running to where I had been working. He found one arm immediately. It was underneath the power take-off shaft, still encased in the sleeve of my insulated shirt, but the other arm was no-where in sight. Rick kept searching and finally concluded the other arm had gone through the auger and ended up in the grain bin.

Tuffy had followed Rick to the grain bin. He was a dog who looked out for both the farm and my family — and he was especially protective of me. Rick was afraid Tuffy might interpret his taking my arm the wrong way.

Rick turned around and started back toward the house when Tuffy started barking. Looking back, he saw that my dog was standing where the other arm had been thrown. It had landed a distance of about a hun-dred feet from where Rick found the first one. He retrieved the second arm, also encased in a sleeve, and started running back to the house fol-lowed closely by Tuffy.

Meanwhile Londa and Joan were getting me ready for the ride to the nearest hospital. They wrapped me in sheets and gave me oxygen. Rick got back to the house and realized he didn't have enough plastic bags to wrap my arms in. They also needed ice, so I was able to tell them where they could find what they needed.

When they were ready to load me on the stretcher we discovered the hallway to the bathroom was too narrow. The stretcher wouldn't fit past the dining room. They weren't sure how they were going to get me to it, especially since they couldn't get a grip beneath my arms.

"I can walk," I offered.

Rick, Joan and Londa were skeptical at first, but with a little help from Renee, that's exactly what I did. Once I was on the stretcher, they wrapped me in blankets and strapped me on.

The sensation of being on the stretcher was unsettling. Every time the thing tilted I felt as though I was going to roll off. Without my arms I had no control of my body position. I remember giving a yell because I thought I was going to get dumped on the ground.

"You're strapped on. You're not going anywhere," Rick reassured me.

"Can Renee ride with me in the ambulance?"

"There's no room, John. I'm really sorry," Joan apologized.

Renee promised to follow us in her car. After I was loaded we began the 26-mile trip to St. Aloisius Hospital in Harvey. The ride seemed to take forever. They didn't have the siren on so I asked them if they would get it going.

"We don't want the extra noise to excite you," Joan explained.

"I don't see how I can get any more excited than I already am," I argued with Joan, but I couldn't convince them to turn it on.

A little while later I asked them how fast we were going. Ambulance speeds are supposed to be restricted to 75 miles per hour on two-lane roads. Joan looked at the speedometer and told Rick to slow down. That got my attention, but I don't think Rick reduced our speed.

As we reached the outskirts of Harvey, the road was really rough. I was able to see through the rear windows to the street as we came into town. I remember there was an old green car in front of us. The driver wouldn't move over. I saw the surprised expression on the driver's face as Rick passed and pulled into the hospital emergency entrance.

Harvey is a community of about 2,500 people. The hospital, St. Aloisius, is not a large facility, but it provides essential services for area residents. It's a constant struggle to keep these rural hospitals going, but without those services many people would have to travel 50 to 100 miles or more for emergency medical care.

I recall being unloaded from the ambulance and transferred inside. It was about 1:15 in the afternoon. Dr. Curt Nyhus was on duty. This wasn't his normal weekend routine. His practice was 110 miles to the southeast in Jamestown, North Dakota – but he was filling in for the regular doctor who happened to be his brother. His beeper called him away from lunch. It had been a slow weekend and he had been enjoying a sandwich while visiting with his mother at a local café.

When Dr. Nyhus answered his beeper he was told, "We've got an amputation victim on the way." At the hospital, emergency room supervising nurse Julie Keller had sprung into action before I arrived. She had activated additional staff and was getting supplies ready.

Given the extent of my injuries, Dr. Nyhus was amazed I was even alive. With my left arm broken off between the elbow and shoulder, and my right arm detached just below the shoulder, he couldn't believe I was still conscious and able to communicate coherently.

"Are you going to make it?" he asked me.

"I came this far. I'm going all the way."

I think he was relieved that I didn't plan on dying on his watch.

An air ambulance was called from Bismarck. The plan was to transfer me by helicopter to the area's primary trauma center, St. Alexius Medical Center, in Bismarck. The emergency staff at Harvey were also trying to help me battle shock. The helicopter was bringing additional blood for me because I was exhausting the emergency supply at the hospital. United Blood Services' Bismarck office keeps hospitals in the central and western part of the state supplied with blood, but rural hospitals only have a limited number of units of varying blood types on hand at any given time. The staff at Harvey weren't sure how I had survived up to this point. I really didn't have enough blood in me to keep me alive.

I found out later that if my arms had not been completely ripped off I certainly would have bled to death. Because the arms were severed, the arteries had naturally closed themselves off to staunch the blood loss. According to my doctors, the body has this protective response to maintain the flow of blood to vital organs like the heart, lungs, kidneys and liver. The cold weather also worked in my favor by slowing the blood flow. Even with these positive factors, Dr. Nyhus estimated about half of the blood in my body had been lost.

Meanwhile, Aunt Renee hadn't been able to follow the ambulance like she promised. As we left the farm, she called ahead to St. Aloisius to alert them about my condition and tell them that the ambulance was en route. Then she started out for the hospital. On the way, she met my Uncle Lynn's vehicle on the road. She waved him over and explained what happened. They agreed that Aunt Renee should try to find my brother Mick who was working in Hurdsfield. Uncle Lynn tried to catch up to the ambulance while Aunt Renae proceeded to Hurdsfield to look for Mick and try to contact my parents at the hospital in Bismarck.

Dreading what she would have to tell my parents, Aunt Renee called the hospital in Bismarck. Instead of my mom and dad, she reached my cousin Kyle. He caught up with my parents outside the hospital. My mom could tell something was seriously wrong as he approached them. Kyle tried to persuade my parents to go inside the hospital, but mom insisted he tell her what was wrong right away.

As they were standing outside the hospital, they could hear the air ambulance taking off from the heliport.

"The helicopter is on its way to get John," Kyle explained.

"What on earth happened?" my mother asked, never imagining the extent of my injuries.

"Apparently John got caught in the power take-off and he lost both his arms," Kyle tried to explain as gently as he could.

My mother collapsed in shock and had to be taken to the emergency room.

While the helicopter was on its way from Bismarck, the trauma team went to work on me. They needed to start an intravenous line, but they had to find a site in one of my feet. Someone cut off my blue jeans. They were just about to start cutting my cowboy boots. I didn't want to sacrifice the most comfortable footwear I owned.

"Hey, just pull the boots off," I yelled.

That's what they did, but they cut my socks and undershorts off. It was quite an experience lying naked on a stretcher surrounded by strangers.

A nurse was making a valiant effort to get the intra-venous catheter inserted in my foot, but all of my veins had collapsed. She kept poking which was quite painful. However, the discomfort was nothing compared with what I felt when another nurse inserted a urinary catheter. I've always considered that area of my anatomy a one-way street.

The first nurse finally got the I.V. going and then they started working on my stumps. They wanted to stop any further blood loss. They kept making contact with the nerve that was hanging out of the right side. It was very much alive and I definitely knew when they were touching it.

By now, the numbness had worn off and I was beginning to feel a lot of discomfort. I was trying to keep my mind off the pain I was experiencing when I noticed a guy bring in a garbage bag. I focused my attention on him as he put the bag on the table beside me, pulled out both of my arms, and placed them on the table. It was a strange experience, sort of cool in a weird sense. I was lying in one spot, and my arms were lying in another where I could see them. I watched the guy scrub them and get them cleaned up. In retrospect, I'm surprised seeing my arms like that didn't make me freak out.

The helicopter arrived but the medical team had already changed the transfer plans. This was due to the quick thinking of Dr. Ron Knutson, the flight doctor from Bismarck. He also happened to be caring for my mother's cousin Michelle Barkow.

On the helicopter flight to Harvey, Dr. Knutson recalled a recent visit to Minneapolis. He'd been talking with a friend who had commented on the pioneering work of a colleague. That work involved limb reattachment. Dr. Knutson knew time was of the essence if an amputated limb was to be saved. While in the air, he called Dr. Nyhus and asked if I was stable enough to be transferred to Minnesota. At about 2 p.m. the decision was made to fly me directly to North Memorial Medical Center in Robbinsdale. It is near Minneapolis and just over 400 miles away from the farm. The hospital had to call for a plane to make the trip, because such a flight was out of range of the helicopter. Of course, the change in plans meant more waiting in Harvey.

A short while later, my parents learned that I was being transferred to a trauma center near Minneapolis. My dad went to the Bismarck airport and got a ticket for the next flight there.

Aunt Renee finally made it to the Harvey hospital. As I waited for the plane that would take me to Minnesota, I visited with her, Uncle Lynn and my cousin Tammy. I was hoping one of them would be able to make the flight with me.

We received word that the airplane had arrived at the Harvey airport and I was loaded into the ambulance and transferred to the plane. I begged the flight crew to let me take one of my relatives along but they explained that the extra weight would slow the plane down. I had to fly without family. We left the Harvey airport at about 3:30 p.m.

It was the second time I had flown, and the first time I'd ever been in a small plane. The flight seemed endless. At least the flight doctor was able to give me medication for pain. That was something the all-volunteer rural ambulance crew was unable to do. But still, I got bored. After some arguing I convinced the air crew to let me sit up so I could enjoy the view.

During the flight I also recall complaining about my arms being cold. I felt as though I was freezing. When I told the flight doctor that my arms felt terribly cold, he said, "But you can't feel your arms because they aren't attached." I argued with him anyway, saying that my arms felt like ice. It was then that the flight crew told me my arms were on ice in the nose of the plane. I asked them to get my arms out and warm them up. Of course, it was better for the tissue to be cooled, so the arms stayed where they were.

As we approached our destination in Minnesota, I told the flight crew I wanted to stay sitting so I could watch our touchdown. They insisted I had to lie down. I know we argued about it, but I think they gave me some medication to calm me because it's difficult to remember the landing or what happened when we arrived at the airport.

Chapter 2
Background

St. Aloisius Hospital in Harvey, North Dakota is where everything began. I was born there on June 6, 1973. There was only one other baby in the nursery at the time, a little boy.

My parents, Larry and Karen, decided to name me "John" after my Grandpa Thompson, and "Wayne" after my Grandpa Hildebrant. The doctor thought it was amusing that this little baby was named "John Wayne" like the tough cowboy in the movies. Just to make sure no one missed the connection, he nicknamed me "Duke." The nickname stuck, so that's what my family and close friends call me.

I came home to my older sister and brother, Kim and Mick. Our family was like a lot of families in that area of North Dakota. Most have Scandinavian or German roots. Many are Lutheran. Most are conservative, frugal and hardworking.

For the first three years of my life, our family lived in town. Home was Hurdsfield, North Dakota, a community of 112 people, give or take a few, on the northern Great Plains. The geographical center of North America is just a few miles away at Rugby, North Dakota. It is literally in the middle of nowhere and yet, on a cloudless night it seems like the center of the universe.

In order to add some local flavor and interest to the prairie landscape, North Dakota boasts a number of man-made oddities. South Dakota has Mount Rushmore, but North Dakota has the World's Largest Holstein (at New Salem), the World's Largest Buffalo (at Jamestown), the World's Largest Sandhill Crane, Wally the 26-foot Walleye, and a host of other larger than life creatures. In the southwest part of the state you can even drive the "Enchanted Highway" which boasts huge sculptures depicting prairie scenes and wildlife.

The area is rural, with nearly half of the population making their living from farming or agriculture-related businesses. People from large cities find it hard to believe that pioneers ever settled in this part of the world. It can be a harsh place to live. To an outsider, the prairie looks especially desolate in late fall, winter, or early spring. When there isn't snow on the ground, everything is tinted in shades of brown and gray. But even in that monochrome landscape there's a lot of variety if you look close enough. Once spring and summer have taken hold, it can be amazingly green. Planting gives way to lush fields, except in those years when drought toasts everything to dried straw. There's also an abundance of wildlife including geese, ducks, pheasant, fox, coyotes and deer.

If you are from a large city, you might think the area is too isolated. With a total population of less than 650,000, much of North Dakota is classified as "frontier" because of its low population density. I prefer to think of it as uncluttered.

Outside of the major cities, schools and churches become the center of small, close-knit communities. While social and cultural opportunities may be limited, people are still willing to look after their neighbors.

Both my parents came from farm families. My great grandparents emigrated from Denmark to homestead in the Dakotas. Back then they had huge farms called "bonanza farms." My Great Grandpa Kyle Hildebrant had one of the biggest operations in the state with several thousand acres until he lost it during the depression. Like most farmers in the area, he took it in stride, worked like hell, and started over.

These days, farmers have it almost as bad as during the depression. The problem doesn't get noticed because the rest of the economy has been strong — and frankly there just aren't that many family farmers left in this country. Unfortunately, the families that are losing their farms now won't get a chance to start over. The so-called emphasis on a market-based economy with less government intervention may have been good for other businesses. It's meant the death of many independent farming operations in North Dakota and other rural states. A whole way of life is being replaced. I may be cynical, but it seems as though family farms are being sacrificed to increase corporate profits.

When I was three, our family moved to a new house on a farm a couple of miles east of Hurdsfield. Our farm always seemed like a safe haven. The home place is at the end of a two-mile gravel road just northeast of Hurdsfield. The house is a comfortable one-story building with an attached double garage on the north side. There are sliding glass doors in the dining room that look out onto the deck and backyard on the west side.

The front of the house overlooks a sizeable pond now. It's actually a lake, but during the 1980s and early 90s conditions were so dry that the lake was only a small marshy area. As you step out the front door of the house onto the east deck, there's a nice view of the water. On days when there is little wind, it's very peaceful and calming. Of course, windy conditions are the norm in North Dakota, so it's not unusual to see white caps on the water. In fact, it's not unheard of to experience hurricane force winds, not to mention the occasional tornado.

I grew up learning the importance of farm chores. Like most farm kids, I was raised with the belief that agriculture was vital because the farmer's job was to feed the world. I admired my dad for what he did. When I was a young child, dad would let me ride with him on the tractor. Occasionally I'd catch a nap at his feet on the floor of the tractor cab because I didn't want to leave until all the fieldwork was done. At the time, no place felt safer than being with dad on the tractor.

When dad was done in the field we were both covered in dirt. Dad got that way from working. I got that way because I would throw dirt on myself so I would look more like him. My parents never did figure out how I got so dirty.

So, I was raised with the belief that family farming wasn't just a job — it was a calling. In North Dakota, many farmers still feel that way, but the realization is slowly dawning that family farming is a vanishing way of life in this country. Most of the farmers from the area are driving truck or renting out their land because they can't keep farming while losing money. I sometimes wonder if anyone, other than the farmers themselves, cares if this country grows its own food anymore.

We raised a variety of crops on our farm including wheat, barley, durum, and confection and oil sunflowers. North Dakota is one of the top grain producing areas in the world, and there was a time when that meant a good income for North Dakota farmers. We also had a sizeable beef cattle herd, and we usually had a couple hundred pigs.

Like a lot of farm kids, my chores came before my schoolwork. It was a matter of economic survival. We couldn't afford hired help and the responsibilities of livestock meant there were a lot of chores, even when we were young children. I believe farming is a good life, at least it seemed that way to me as a child and teenager, even if it is a difficult way to feed a family. It's ironic, that the farmer who feeds the world should struggle to feed his own family.

Farmers know a lot about economic peaks and valleys. The occupation is so easily affected by everything from the weather to international economics. There are a lot of risks involved, and only a few of them are safety risks.

I can remember the drought years in the late 1980s and early 90s. The land returned to dust bowl conditions with the vegetation drying up, and the topsoil blowing away. There wasn't enough moisture for the seed to germinate or grow. Without a decent crop we couldn't afford to feed the livestock. It was so bad that a national news crew came to tape the conditions and used our farm as an example of what was happening to farmers on the Great Plains.

At one time, my parents owned nearly 3,800 acres of land. The drought forced my dad to sell down to 3,000 and then he cut back to 1,800 acres. Eventually, with low crop prices there wasn't enough yield from 1,800 acres to make any money. In fact, we were operating in the negative.

The memory of my mom crying at Christmas time during the drought years has never left me. Mom has always tried to make the holidays special, and it was very upsetting to her that there wasn't much under the tree during those years. She didn't want us to know how scared she was about finances, but she just couldn't hold it all in.

In spite of the tough times, I don't recall that we ever went without anything we needed. If anything, we took a lot of pride in what we had because we worked so hard for it.

During the drought years I developed the attitude that you could survive anything if you did your best and you didn't give up. It was a valuable lesson — perhaps one of the most important I learned during my childhood. There are so many things in life you can't control. We certainly couldn't control the weather. But if we could find the strength to ride it out, we were usually better off for it.

Actually, some of my best memories are of times when Mother Nature showed us her wild side. On the prairie you can have exotic sunsets one day, and rolling electrical storms the next — but winter weather can really show you extremes.

We celebrated a big family Christmas one year with aunts, uncles and cousins at our house. There was a terrific winter storm. The wind whipped snow into drifts that resembled a moonscape. Everyone was snowbound at our place for seven days. Just to make it interesting, the power was out. Heavy ice had coated the electrical lines and the extra weight combined with the force of the wind tore many of the lines down. We pulled mattresses off the beds and brought them into the dining room and living room. We told stories, played games and camped out until the roads were open. It's one of my favorite childhood memories. Dad always refers to that Christmas as the time when we were the "Thompson Hilton."

The farm gives a person a different perspective on life and death. For one thing, you learn to tell the changing of the seasons just from the smells and the sounds around you. The almost sterile smell of winter gives way to a damp earthy smell. There are the sounds of lambing season, which segue into calving season. Then there is the smell of new plant growth. On a still day you can stand in a field of sunflowers or corn and literally hear the plants grow. In mid-summer you can smell the heat baking the ground and sucking the moisture out of the growing plants.

Autumn brings the sounds and smells of harvest and the first frost brings the chill of death. Eventually the vegetation rots or dries up.

Children who grow up in town might never see an animal give birth or die. Growing up on a farm, you learn that livestock have a purpose based on the life cycle. Small farmers understand the relationship between animals and the success of their business. Unlike huge confinement operations, which basically warehouse animals, small farmers know each individual animal. The well-being of each cow, sheep, pig or other animal is important. You don't look at losing a dozen pigs or even one pig as "the cost of doing business." You take it hard, like a personal failure.

I was fond of caring for the livestock, and especially the cattle. Sometimes we had orphaned animals and it was a challenge to raise them until they were weaned. Every year, from the time we were old enough, each of us children also purchased a calf with our own money. These calves had to be bottle-fed. We got up early each morning to feed our respective animals and care for them, and we'd have to feed them again at night. It was a big responsibility and one we carried until the animals were mature enough to sell.

I didn't view taking care of my calf as just another chore. That calf became a companion animal and I unavoidably became attached to it. I loved my calves like any other pets. When I looked into their liquid eyes, I could see they trusted me and became attached to me in return. The relationship was no different than what most people have with their dog or cat, except calves are strictly outdoor animals.

I'd spend a lot of time with the animals I raised. Sometimes the calf would let me ride him like you would ride a horse. It was especially relaxing to wander out to the pasture and catch a nap with my calf letting me use him as a big pillow.

I learned a lot about life from raising livestock, although I'm not sure I always understood the lesson the way I was supposed to. You start out with a young animal that's completely dependent on you, and you raise that animal into a nice size cow or steer. A relationship develops. You talk to that animal as you care for it, and it knows your voice and trusts you. Eight months after you started, you have to sell your companion. That part always bothered me, especially when I found out my cow or steer was going to slaughter and I might even be eating this animal that had been my friend.

Despite the outcome for the animal, there was still a close relationship while I was raising it. I was concerned for my calves' welfare, and in the end the welfare of my family was linked to how well I cared for those animals. It was a valuable lesson in responsibility, something that can't be learned from huge factory farming operations.

Growing up around livestock and large machinery it's easy to forget that farming is one of the world's most dangerous occupations. Every day you live with the possibility that an accident can happen. You can try to minimize the risk, but there are certain dangers inherent in the operation. I grew up watching my dad at work in the field and dreaming of the day when I'd get to work along side him. It took me a while to appreciate how hazardous it could be.

One of the luxuries of living on the farm is that you get to do some things long before your city counterparts. Take driving for instance. Most city kids don't learn until they take driver's education in high school. Dad started teaching me how to drive when I was around seven years old. At least you have wide open spaces in the country. It makes learning to drive a lot less intimidating if you don't have to worry about other traffic.

Dad took me out to a field so I wouldn't hit anything. The first few driving lessons went pretty well. My only problem was that I couldn't remember how to stop once we got going. Eventually I got the hang of it, in spite of some driving lessons from my big brother.

Mick, as big brothers will sometimes do, decided to show off during one of our driving sessions. He was demonstrating how to swerve from one side of the road to another. I thought it was pretty cool, even after he demonstrated how to drive the pickup into the slough. For city folks, a slough (pronounced "slew") is a marshy area which is usually filled with shallow water. Dad was not very happy about having the front end of the pickup submerged, but I thought it was a neat trick.

Before long, I mastered driving to the point that I was helping when we moved machinery from one field to another. Dad would let me follow behind in the pickup. Even though I considered it a luxury, learning to drive is a necessity on the farm — and as with all farm work, there is an element of danger.

By the time I was nine, I was operating a small tractor and picking rocks in the field. This may sound like a simple task, but experience teaches you the fine points of shifting gears. When I was ten I had a frightening experience pulling the rock picker uphill out of a steep ditch.

I made the mistake of keeping the tractor in high gear when I should have geared down. The tractor didn't have enough power to make the incline, so it stalled. My legs weren't long enough to allow me to depress the clutch and the brake simultaneously while I attempted to restart the engine, so I put the tractor in neutral and held the brake to keep from rolling backwards into the ditch.

When I got the engine going again, I had to shift into low. In order to depress the clutch I had to release the brake, and when I let go of the brake I started rolling backwards. At that point things went out of control.

I popped the clutch out with the tractor rolling backwards into the ditch, and it stalled again. As the machine continued its backward course, it started to roll over on its top. I was thrown out of my seat landing on the ground alongside the tractor as it tipped. With no time to move I was lying in the ditch, watching the tractor poised to roll over on me. I would have been crushed, but fortunately the rock picker added enough counterweight to pull the tractor back onto its wheels.

Then it was over, and I was standing up looking at fuel leaking from the gas cap and thinking, "I sure don't want to tell dad I nearly wrecked the tractor."

When I told my father what had happened, he was really happy I wasn't hurt. After the shock wore off, he was upset and let me know it. Under the circumstances his reaction was a normal combination of relief and fear.

When I was eleven, I started working in the field with our 900

Versatile four-wheel drive tractor. This was heavy-duty machinery and I was proud to be entrusted with it. I was pulling a 47-foot cultivator, which is the equipment that turns the soil and breaks up the weeds.

Most non-farm people don't know that farming involves a lot of chemistry, too. By the time I was 13, I was putting down chemicals such as pesticides, herbicides, and fertilizers.

Should children be doing such hazardous work? It's a good question. In other industries there are laws about exposing children to workplace hazards. It's true, farming is especially dangerous for kids — but the reality is that on a family farm the success of the operation depends on all members of the family doing their part. There are also a lot of things farmers can do to make the job safer. Unfortunately they don't always take the necessary precautions.

In my opinion, farm work provided me with a good work ethic. I was never afraid to earn a few dollars shoveling snow, mowing lawns or raking leaves. I honestly thank my parents for giving me the opportunity to grow up and work on the farm. I think it made me a better person and though some people will laugh at the suggestion that I'm responsible, I think it made me a more responsible adult.

I don't believe there is harm in making young people work hard or take responsibility in a family business. I know too many kids who complain about being bored and then start getting into trouble. I was one of those kids from time to time myself. I'm not advocating for the exploitation of children. I just think there are a lot of people in this country who grow up expecting life owes them something. If parents would take more time to work side by side with their children, it might teach kids something about the value of work.

As I mentioned, as hard as I worked, I still managed to find time to get into trouble. Early on, I earned a reputation for getting into mischief, especially when I spent time with my cousin Todd.

Todd is my mother's twin sister's son. We're only three weeks apart in age. When we were young, people mistook us for twin brothers instead of cousins. Of course, we all have childhood incidents that our parents can use as fodder for blackmail when we're adults. Todd and I, however, gave our parents a wealth of material. I know if I ever have children my parents are looking forward to repaying me by telling my kids all about my childhood exploits.

For instance, Todd and I once dug up a big skunk my grandfather had shot and buried at his farm. We were visiting our grandparents at the time and we kept pestering grandpa to tell us where he buried the skunk. He never imagined what we had in mind. We weren't deterred by the smell, but then we smelled so much like the skunk by the time it was dug up, that we probably didn't notice the difference. We tied a rope around the carcass and dragged it up to the house. Needless to say, no one was impressed with our prize, except my grandmother who thought it was cute. She brought us watermelon because we stunk so bad we weren't allowed inside the house. Obviously, there isn't a lot to do on a farm, but our families encouraged us to find other ways to entertain ourselves in the future.

Then there was the time when Grandma was butchering chickens. My mother has never been fond of anything with feathers. Knowing this, I collected chicken heads and stuck them on my fingers. I walked up to my mother and thrust my hand in her direction nearly scaring her to death.

Getting into trouble became even easier when I got my driver's license. In North Dakota, farm kids usually get their drivers' permits when they are only fourteen. Even though I'd been driving off-road since I was seven or eight, I savored driving more once I became a legal motor vehicle operator. Cruising the country roads around Hurdsfield, I was free.

My first car was a 1976 Chevy Monza hatchback. It was handed down from my sister Kim. The best thing about that car, at least from my perspective, was its power. I knew how to make its 265 V-8 engine do what it was designed to do. That was a lot of punch packed into a small car. The thrill of racing was too much to resist. I drove that car hard, very hard, and I never backed down from a challenge to race. I knew I could win every time. From then on, the faster I drove the better. Sure, I got in trouble for driving the way I did, and for a few other things, too. Dad wasn't overly concerned about it. To his way of thinking, I wasn't doing anything worse than things he had done at my age. My mom, however, had an opposing viewpoint. She "never did anything like that" when she was the same age, or so she claimed. Of course, I learned you can always get the real story about your parents by asking your grandparents.

Naturally, my mom and dad were primarily concerned for my welfare. When I got in trouble, and they got upset, it was because they were watching out for me. They're still protective of me, especially my mother. I imagine they will be that way until they die, or I die. I resisted what I saw as their interference then, but I cope with it now. Sometimes I still have to remind them that I'm an adult and can take care of myself. I know it would have been easier for my parents if I hadn't had the accident. It altered the way we interact as a family. So, I can't really fault my parents for caring.

When I entered high school I was incredibly shy. I was secure in my own home and on my own turf, but away from that setting was different. Most of my classmates thought I enjoyed being a loner. I was so used to being by myself, I didn't really understand the intricacies of socializing.

You see, up until the time I entered high school I attended the grade school in Hurdsfield. For most of those years I was the only student in my class. Finally, in the seventh grade, I got a classmate named Michelle. She became my first girlfriend.

Michelle and I entered high school at the consolidated school in Bowdon. We joined nine other students in the freshman class. The high school had less than sixty students in grades nine to twelve and I wasn't used to interacting with such a large crowd. Attending a high school with hundreds of students in each grade would have been terribly intimidating.

It got better with time. Some of the classmates I felt least comfortable with in the beginning, later became my best friends. Of course, in a school that small it's impossible not to know everything about everybody.

When I look back at the person I was in high school, the contrast with who I am today is incredible. I was absolutely lacking in self-confidence. I had never been a serious student, and it was difficult for me to express what I wanted to say or to tell someone how to solve a problem. If I was called upon in class, I was usually stymied. Then I'd become even more self-conscious.

Actually, I was a hands-on learner. I could take something apart and put it back together. I could demonstrate how to do the same thing but I couldn't explain things verbally. I also did much better if someone showed me how to do something rather than reading about it or having it explained. People who know me now find it surprising that I wasn't very verbal.

I'd give anything to do my high school years over. I would make an effort to be more outgoing and confident. I'd go out for sports. As it was, I felt really insecure in high school. And some people actually told me I was stupid, or treated me that way. It was hard because high school is a time when you try to define yourself. I decided to establish my own identity as the school "party animal." I had a supplier who could get alcohol for me, so I found a niche as the school supplier. That wasn't anything unusual. If you weren't in sports, and weren't academically inclined, there weren't a lot of other activities available.

In retrospect, I realize it was wrong to be so casual about drinking, but alcohol use was prevalent among people in my age group at that time. Now days, drugs are as significant a problem with high school students as alcohol. People like to believe drugs haven't impacted small towns, but drugs have been around for some time and rural areas aren't immune. If anything, denying the problem has only made it worse. I think the local authorities would agree rural areas have been especially susceptible to methamphetamine. Meth producers like to find abandoned farm buildings to set up their manufacturing labs, and North Dakota has plenty of abandoned farms.

Regarding my own drinking, it wasn't that I was trying to impress anyone. I didn't really care what anybody thought about me. But, I could drink and I enjoyed doing it. At parties, my inhibitions would be down, and I'd say whatever I wanted. But we never had the type of parties where we trashed someone's home or went on a crime spree.

Aside from parties and racing, the only other time I enjoyed drawing attention to myself was when I was singing. My dad likes to sing, but I think I inherited my musical streak from my mother. I started singing in choir when I was in the seventh grade. I was especially fond of Miss Zenker, my music teacher.

Some teachers approach their students with the attitude that the students have to learn about the subject if they want to advance, and the teacher doesn't care if the students advance or not. It's just another chore. Miss Zenker knew how to make music interesting. She inspired me to want to learn more.

Before seventh grade I'd sung in church a couple of times for funerals. Miss Zenker gave me the chance to sing solo parts. She had a knack for building my confidence. I think she was the teacher that had the biggest impact on me because she took the time to work with me. She was also interested in finding out what I wanted to know. She believed in me, and that faith seemed to bring out the best in me.

Every year our school competed in regional music contests in Valley City, North Dakota. Miss Zenker would have me sing a solo for contest, and even though I never got a perfect score, she continued to encourage me. She also had me sing for Christmas concerts or the spring chorale, which we called the Brevity Concert.

Music was always a link for me. It helped me relax and it helped me come out of my shell. When I sang for different occasions, it was something significant I could contribute.

In high school I considered music as one career option. I was also interested in flying and thought about pursuing a career as a commercial pilot, but unlike my childhood dreams I never really thought about staying on the farm.

As I grew older, I saw how hard my parents worked. They struggled just to break even. Much of the time, things weren't even that good. In addition, by the time I was in junior in high school, I had developed a serious rebellious streak. There was a lot of conflict between my father and me. I knew we could never operate the farm together because both of us would have to be in charge. There would be lots of differences of opinion about how to run things. I was also bored with small town living, and I wanted a change of scenery.

The summer following my junior year I decided to travel with a custom combining crew out of Oklahoma. My brother and two of my cousins had harvested with the operation years before, so I knew it was a decent crew. My parents agreed it would be good work experience.

I left as soon as school let out. We started harvesting in Oklahoma and slowly worked our way north to the wheat fields of Montana. I didn't get home until just before the start of my senior year.

I learned a lot that summer, and I think I matured considerably. For the first time, I had to take care of myself and do things like washing my own clothes. It was hard work, but it was also teamwork. There were seven of us living out of a little trailer with one bathroom and one laundry room. I learned how important it was to get along with others, and even though it was the toughest work I'd ever done, I would do it again if I could.

When I got home at the end of harvest I bought a better car. My faithful Monza had already been replaced after I blew its engine. Its successor was an Oldsmobile Cutlass Supreme. I used my summer earnings to replace the Cutlass with a two-door Honda Accord hatchback and listed the Cutlass for sale. Of course, I had a lot of fun with the Honda, too.

When school started, I regaled my classmates with stories about my harvesting experiences. They were probably sick of hearing me talk about it, but they humored me. I also joined the staff of the school year book.

There were twelve of us on the staff, including eleven girls. I didn't mind being outnumbered under the circumstances. Because I enjoyed taking pictures, my assignment was photographer. It was a lot of fun and I also considered taking photography in college. I was still interested in flying, and considered a job in the airline industry, too. Of course, I had no way of knowing that events would dramatically change my plans and my life.

Chapter 3
North Memorial

The plane landed at Crystal Airport in Minnesota at about 5:30 p.m. It would have taken close to seven hours had I traveled the entire distance by ground. While I was being transferred from the airplane to a waiting ambulance, I noticed it felt a lot colder in Minnesota than it was when we left the Harvey airport. Aside from that, I don't recall much about the ride to North Memorial Medical Center.

By now, the staff at North Memorial was ready for what would be one of the most severe amputation cases they had yet seen. I was unloaded at the trauma center and wheeled into emergency. There was quite a crowd waiting for me.

I was scared and it unnerved me even more to be confronted with so many strangers. All of them were standing around in their white coats and writing on charts. In addition to emergency physician Mark Berg, there were a number of interns. I wanted them all to get out of the room. Someone explained they wanted to "study" my injuries. I told them that I wanted them out, and most of them obliged me.

Moments later I had my first meeting with the person who would be my principle doctor. His name was Dr. Allen Van Beek. By now he'd been briefed about the extent of my injuries and was formulating a plan for my surgery. It would be the fourth double arm replantation of his career.

My arms hadn't been sliced off in a clean amputation. They had literally been pulled off, and parts of the anatomy were barely recognizable. Dr. Van Beek considered my age, and what my life would be like without my arms. The options were limited.

All the other white coats left the room so the doctor could have a private discussion with me. He came right to the point about the alternatives.

"There are two things we can do," he said. "We can put your arms back on, or we can leave them off."

There it was. It seemed like a straightforward decision.

"I'm here," I said. "Let's put them on."

I didn't want this to be a wasted trip. Then Dr. Van Beek told me what my decision would mean, so I could back out if I wanted.

"Reattaching your arms will mean a much longer hospital stay," he informed me. "There will be an increased risk of infection. It will likely mean years of therapy with no guarantee that you'll regain function — and there's still the risk that you might lose one or both of your arms if there are complications. In the worst case, you might even lose your life."

"Let's go ahead with it," I said. I didn't want to consider going through life without my arms.

"Do you need my parents' signature or anything?" I asked.

"You're eighteen years old. That's all the consent we need."

Even though he had explained the risks, I don't think I fully understood what I was getting into. How could anyone fully comprehend the consequences of such a decision?

I did know enough to be scared.

"I don't want to go into surgery until my folks get here," I tried to stall.

"We don't have the luxury of waiting," he said. "Every minute we delay reduces the chance the surgery will be successful."

The staff would have to get me ready immediately if my arms were to be saved. Fortunately, before I had time to have second thoughts, my dad walked into the room. It was less than ten minutes after my arrival in the North Memorial emergency room.

My dad and I visited briefly before my gurney was wheeled to the surgical area. I could tell he was just as scared as I was, but he kept reassuring me that everything would be all right. I was especially worried about my mother and how this would affect her. My cousins Kyle and Tim had driven her back to Hurdsfield from the hospital in Bismarck to pack some belongings. She didn't know the extent of my injuries or what the treatment plan was. I figured she'd be worried or even frantic, especially after seeing the amount of blood around the house.

Three teams were assigned to the actual surgery, one for each arm and one for me. Two plastics/micro-surgery specialists would deal with replanting my injured arms. Dr. Van Beek was one, and Dr. Bart Muldowney was the other. Orthopedic surgeon Joseph Bocklage and anesthesiologist David Schultz were also part of the team.

Dr. Van Beek was a Viet Nam veteran. It was his military experience that had sparked his interest in microsurgery and reconstructive surgery. He was also from North Dakota where he had taken his first two years of medical training at the University of North Dakota School of Medicine from 1964 to 1966.

The surgery began at about 6:30 p.m. It was grueling, not for me but for the doctors and the surgical teams. Each limb has over 30 bones. Fortunately, I had only three bone breaks. Both of the upper arms had breaks of the humerus. There was also a break in the ulna of my right forearm. Again, each arm had its own surgical team, with a third team assigned to me. Dr. Van Beek worked on my left arm while Dr. Muldowney worked on the right.

Their first task was to repair the bones. The sharp ends could tear tissue and cause further damage. The surgeons bolted the bones of the detached limbs back on to the stumps using metal brackets and screws. The salvage process meant my arms were now two and a half inches shorter. Once the bones were stabilized, the teams worked at reattaching a blood vessel in each arm. Establishing blood flow bought time by preventing tissue death.

Reattaching muscles and tendons was more complicated. Many of the muscles of the upper arm and shoulder are also attached to the chest and back. There are nine major muscles involved in shoulder and humerus movement, and another five muscles, which allow the elbow to move. Because of the tearing that occurred with my injury, the surgeons had to assess what could be saved, what couldn't, and what might be used in place of something else. It wasn't a precise process of reattaching parts to their original locations.

Then came the ultimate challenge, attaching nerves and restoring full circulation. There are two basic types of nerve functions in limbs, sensory and motor, that provide us with feeling and movement. The interaction of these two nerve functions is essential. Imagine having movement, without the ability to sense pressure, texture, and temperature.

Nerve cells have a body with extensions known as dendrites that receive impulses, and axons that transmit impulses. Mature nerve cells don't reproduce, so you don't grow a replacement if one dies. However it is possible for the axon, which is a long filament, to regenerate. Axon regeneration is a very slow process and the chance of success decreases with the amount of gap between the cut ends.

Rather than making individual nerve connections, the surgeons tried to align the cut nerve endings in my severed limbs as closely as possible to nerve endings in the stumps. They could identify severed nerve bundles or "fascicles" easier than attempting to identify individual nerve connections. Each fascicle has 5000 to 8000 of these nerve connections and it wouldn't have been practical to try to make so many microscopic connections anyway. With the fascicles aligned closely, they could only hope that axon growth would ultimately reestablish the nerve connections. It would be weeks before anyone would know if their work was successful.

Finally Dr. Van Beek and Dr. Muldowney reached the point where they were ready to restore full blood supply to my arms. Using needles that were finer than a human hair, they stitched blood vessels together. If this phase of the operation had been unsuccessful, all of their previous work would have gone down the drain.

That first surgery lasted over six hours and required about 30 units (each unit is 450 milliliters or close to one pint) of blood, but Dr. Van Beek and Dr. Muldowney achieved their goal. I had a strong pulse in both arms.

I went from surgery and recovery, to the Intensive Care Unit. Maintaining blood flow to my fingers, hands and arms proved to be an ongoing struggle that would require additional surgeries.

My mother arrived the day after my accident on January 12th. On the drive to our house with my mother, my cousins stopped in Steele, a small town forty miles outside of Bismarck. Tim was trying to stall the return trip so the family friends who were cleaning our house could complete the job before my mother got home. They were afraid if she saw all of the blood in the house, she'd go into shock again.

My mother didn't know how long we'd be away from home, and there was no way for her to prepare for the situation. After she got home, she packed a few belongings for herself, my dad and me. My mom's sister Joanne joined them, and then they all drove to my sister's house in Fargo. From Fargo they proceeded to Robbinsdale in two cars. My sister Kim, her husband Stuart, my Aunt Joanne and mom rode in one car. Tim and Kyle were in the other.

The first time she saw me, my mother couldn't believe the person lying in the bed was her son. I can remember looking at my feet and noticing they were horribly swollen. Apparently, so was everything else, including my face. My skin was taut and shiny, an effect of the circulatory problems and the trauma.

I was heavily medicated for some time after the surgery. They brought me out of it slowly. When I finally was awake enough to recognize people, the first person I noticed standing by my bed was my mother.

"Mom," I said, "I'm sorry."

She fought hard to hold back tears.

None of us — my family, the hospital staff or myself, were prepared for the way the media and the public reacted as the story about my mishap spread. Back in North Dakota local word of mouth had spread the news of my accident very quickly. Within hours, the rumor that I was dead had circulated among my high school classmates and to the many small towns around Hurdsfield.

My sister Kim wanted people to know the facts. She contacted North Dakota's largest newspaper, the Fargo Forum. She told the paper that I had survived and had been sent to a trauma center in the Minneapolis area for specialized emergency treatment. The local wire services decided to carry the story of how I had managed to save myself, and soon the account spread to the Minneapolis media. Once that happened, the news literally went everywhere. Perhaps because there had been less than ten similar surgery cases worldwide, the story became national and then international news.

I don't recall being in pain and my recollection of those first days after the accident is very sketchy, but there is a lot I can recall. I know my family was as scared as I was. I spent many hours worrying and wondering if my parents would have to sell our farm to pay my hospital bills. It bothered me to think of my family having to face financial disaster and to know how worried they were about me.

It didn't help knowing that after all this, I could still lose my arms. We had numerous scares and close calls. My arms would become unbearably cold, an indication that blood circulation was compromised. Into surgery I'd go to correct the problem. It was quite an ordeal, and each surgery seemed like a setback. I don't recall who made the connection that my arm temperature dropped when I was left alone in the room. The hospital arranged to have someone with me, either family or staff, around the clock.

At one point the doctors thought they would have to remove one of my arms. They were worried it was dying and would only keep me from getting well. I insisted we had to find some way to let me keep it. Infection, as Dr. Van Beek had warned me, was part of the problem. Within those first two weeks I developed a life-threatening staph infection. Staphyllococcus bacteria are a very serious threat to any surgical patient. Many strains are resistant to antibiotics, so it was fortunate we were able to beat the infection. At any rate, I guess I talked them out of removing the arm, and to everyone's relief it started to get better.

At this stage of recovery I needed a lot of quiet and rest. It seemed like there were a lot of obstacles to getting it. Normally, a hospital can be rather hectic. They wake you up to check your vital signs. They wake you up to give you medication. Sometimes they wake you up to see if you are sleeping well.

They were also remodeling at North Memorial and there was a lot of banging on the steel girders that supported the building. The noise reverberated throughout my room. I recall not being able to get to sleep because of all the hammering. It was terribly distracting. At one point, I was lying in bed crying because the noise was unbearable. The nurses found me a pair of earplugs, but that didn't help. If I was already asleep before the hammering started, the noise didn't wake me up. The nurses asked if the construction crew could delay the heavy work until I had already fallen asleep. Eventually the hospital decided to alter the remodeling schedule.

My family and I couldn't believe it when we started hearing from people all over the world. Within hours of my accident newspapers in Europe, Japan, Australia, Africa, and even Iraq were calling me a hero. The media continued to provide updates on my progress and setbacks.

Letters of support started pouring into the mailroom at North Memorial. Many of them were written in foreign languages and my mother sent the letters out to be translated. Numerous fundraising events such as spaghetti dinners, benefit dances and charity auctions were organized on my behalf. A fund was also set up at our local bank, The First State Bank of Goodrich, North Dakota.

The notoriety created a crowd control problem at the hospital. I was still in Intensive Care and I was also quarantined to prevent infection. Visitors, including my own family and the medical staff, had to observe isolation precautions. This meant they had to put on sterile gowns, gloves, caps, and masks before they entered my room. That didn't stop the parade of people who were drawn by the news accounts of my accident.

We even had a surprise visit from some gang members. Apparently there had been a huge gang clash in the Chicago area. Some injured gang members had been transferred to North Memorial for safety reasons — probably so they wouldn't be the targets of a hit in a local hospital. Some of their gang "friends" showed up at my door because they were curious.

There was also a nightmarish procession of priests, pastors and rabbis, and every other person who thought their special relationship with their version of God could help me. There were guys who pretended they were clergymen and said they wanted to offer support. Ignoring the fact that I was in the intensive care unit and in isolation, people would charge into my room and start praying over me. At one point, someone was giving me the last rites. I was heavily medicated and actually thought I was dead because of it.

All these "well-meaning" people could have killed me with their good intentions. They didn't understand the precautions had been ordered to protect me (and other patients) from germs because I was at high risk for infection. I question how "connected" to God these people actually were. No doubt, some were looking for notoriety of their own and just wanted to be a part of "The John Thompson Story."

At first, my family and I were polite when visitors would find their way into my room. But it didn't take me long to start despising these self-righteous do-gooders. They were worse than the gang members. The last rites were the last straw. Even though I'd been told at an earlier point that I only had a fifteen percent chance of living, I wasn't planning on dying. So I started screaming, "Get these people away from me!" whenever an uninvited guest entered my room.

The hospital began posting security outside my door to keep strangers away. Even that didn't deter them. The lengths people would go to were amazing. The bolder ones would lie and say they were close friends, or worse yet, they'd pretend to be family. It was despicable. Some of these so-called clergy people were even indignant when they weren't allowed in. They seemed to think they were entitled to visit me like I was some public commodity. The only clergyman we allowed to visit was Jack Carlson, the hospital chaplain, who became a family friend.

To this day, I'm very wary of religious people who want to meet me because they believe "God has a purpose" for me. Too many of these people have their own designs about what I can do for them. I think it is possible to discern someone who is a true believer from someone who is flouting their salvation like a club of superiority. However, many people truly believe they know God's will and feel they have the right to impose their interpretation of it on others. They don't take into consideration that a lot of my energy is directed towards being able to function independently, and to maintaining my physical strength. I simply don't have the psychological or emotional resources to be part of someone's self-serving plan.

Communicating with family by telephone became a huge logistical problem, too. My mom would try to call my sister in Fargo and would be unable to get through because so many people were calling Kim. There were numerous phone calls from people pretending to be my sister. It took the hospital a while to devise a system for sorting out the pretenders. At the same time, they wouldn't put our family doctor through when he called from Harvey.

Eventually, hospital security got better at watching out for us. It was an adjustment for everyone, and some of the hospital staff resented the disruption caused by the media attention and security requirements.

Some of the nurses were afraid to care for me. As my mom says, "John was the patient that you didn't want to have any screw-ups with." The media would have made a big deal over it. Then, there were some staff who thought I was getting special treatment and resented it. One nurse told me, "You aren't any better than any other patient." It hadn't occurred to me that I was. I was aware that I was getting special treatment because of all the media attention, but it wasn't something I had asked for or demanded. In fact, it wasn't anything I had any control over.

By Tuesday, January 14th my condition had improved sufficiently that I was downgraded from "critical" to "serious." My sister Kim was able to give the media the news that Dr. Van Beek was optimistic I'd have movement of my arms down to my elbows. But I still had a long way to go. They originally estimated it might be 18 months to two years before I had sensation in my hands. Without feeling, my hands wouldn't really function. Eighteen months to two years seemed like a terribly long time to wait.

My brother Mick was at the hospital while I was in isolation. His job as a truck driver brought him to Minneapolis two times a week, so he would come to visit. I don't think I ever realized how much my older brother cared about me and loved me until I was in the hospital. He would patiently brush my teeth, or gently wash my face. More important, he helped pass the time and provided a good deal of comic relief. For him, just trying to get into his gown and gloves was quite a show.

My room had glass walls and I could see him struggling to get himself dressed before he came in. Mick is a big human and he had a hell of a hard time making his hands fit in the rubber gloves. He'd stick his hand in the glove and his fingers would go right through it. I think a good share of my hospital bill went toward all the gloves he ripped.

We also had fun with my air bed. Mick would sit or push on a spot and that would make me bounce up in the bed. He had to be careful not to bounce me out. Mick could always make me laugh, even when he wasn't trying to cheer me up.

There were plenty of tears, too. It wasn't surprising to see my mom cry, but with my dad it was a different story. My dad came in one time and sat by my bed. He didn't want me to see him crying, but he couldn't help it.

When I asked him what was wrong he said, "I wish it was me in that bed and not you."

"You're not strong enough to be here," I tried to tell him.

I regret those words to this day. I don't know what possessed me to say it. I just thought it was better it was me that had been injured instead of him. In truth, I had the advantage of youth and I doubt he would have survived the same situation.

My mom did everything she could to be encouraging. She heard the Bette Midler song "The Wind Beneath My Wings" one day and thought it expressed her feelings about our ordeal. She called one of the Minneapolis radio stations and asked them to dedicate it to me. Because we were from North Dakota, she didn't realize she had called a talk radio station.

Even though the station didn't play any music, they sent some-one out to purchase the tape. They started a tradition of playing "The Wind Beneath My Wings" daily at a certain time for me. The song took on special significance and word spread about how it was being played for me. Pretty soon I started getting tapes recorded by individual children and even entire schools who were singing the song for me.

Northwest Airlines picked up on the theme, too. They sent me a model airplane with the inscription, "John, may you always find the wind beneath your wings. Your friends at Northwest Airlines."

One of my favorite bands, Guns 'n Roses, was performing in Minneapolis while I was in the ICU. They called the hospital and asked if they could come see me. You can imagine how excited I was about the opportunity to meet them. The timing didn't work though. I was rushed into emergency surgery before they got there, but they brought me autographed headbands, wristbands, t-shirts and compact discs. I eventually got to see them when they came to Fargo in the fall of that year, after I'd gone home. They sent concert tickets for my friends and me.

Like I said before, the stay at the hospital was scary. I had never been so vulnerable or helpless before, and my family was also vulnerable.

You have to remember I was only 18 years old. I'd never been in the hospital before and I had a lot of time to think about my future. From where I was in isolation, it didn't look very good.

Frankly, the prospect of not being able to do the things I wanted to do wasn't attractive. I didn't want to be dependent on my family or anyone. I also didn't want to be a freak — and there were a lot of things in life I had yet to experience. I was afraid of the limitations my injuries might put on my life and my family's.

While I was in the ICU, simple things were an ordeal. If you've never been able to give yourself a bath, you probably can't appreciate what it's like to lie in a hospital bed and have someone else bathe you.

Hospital beds aren't comfortable. The mattresses are plastic-covered and hot. I felt like I was sweating to death most of the time. Even the special air mattress I had to prevent bedsores was hot. It was also incredibly noisy because it used forced air to stay inflated.

I was on a respirator to assist my breathing for the first three or four days of my ICU stay. During one of my bed baths they rolled me over onto the respirator hose. I couldn't breathe momentarily and all sorts of buzzers started sounding. Doctors and nurses came running into my room with expressions of alarm. They thought I was going into respiratory arrest.

My family was in the room, and thought something horrible really had happened. Actually, it was just an accident and I was completely unharmed. I felt sorry for the poor nurse who had turned me. She kept apologizing and I knew she hadn't meant to do it. You could also tell she felt really bad about upsetting my family.

Writing about the bath also reminds me of my first sponge bath. It was refreshing to get cleaned up after lying there covered in perspiration. It was also extremely embarrassing. I mean, I was eighteen years old and there was nothing wrong with my hormones. I won't go into details, but I think you can figure out what happened.

Nurses must receive special training on how to handle such situations. They tell their patients, "Those types of involuntary responses are normal," and they don't even bat an eye. It wasn't something I'd anticipated, however, so I was more than a little embarrassed.

Most of the nurses were very understanding about what I was going through. While it was reassuring to have my family there, I was trying very hard not to let them see how scared I was. When they would leave, the dam would burst and all my emotions would come pouring out. I would cry until I was exhausted because I was so scared. The nurses were very sensitive and caring. They would comfort me and do everything they could to keep me calm and comfortable.

Well, there is always an exception. I had one nurse who happened to be a former Army nurse. She was supposed to insert a nasogastric tube. That's basically a hose they stick in your nose and advance until it's in your stomach. Even on a good day, with a gentle and experienced nurse, it feels like having a garden hose shoved up your nose and then into your throat.

When the nurse told me what she was going to do, I was terrified. I didn't want to go through it.

"Quit acting like a baby," she said. "You're eighteen years old.

All these other nurses are treating you like a spoiled baby, but I'm not. Now, when I stick this tube down your nose, swallow and it will go down easier."

So, I started swallowing.

She stopped shoving the tube when she was only about halfway down and said, "Quit swallowing so much."

I started crying. The nurse just shoved the tube in the rest of the way and left the room.

At that point I yelled for one of the other nurses and told her what had happened. The Army nurse could have used some lessons in therapeutic communication. Needless to say, the only time I saw her again was when they made her come in to apologize.

I wish I could remember more about the other nurses in the ICU. Most of them were so good to me. I know we had a real bond because they shared so much of what I was going through. But, because of the medication and the trauma, a lot of my memory is fuzzy.

With all the circulatory problems in my arms, maintaining temperature continued to be a challenge. Removing the dressings could cause them to lose heat and it was difficult to warm them up again. Just like when we learned that having someone in the room with me helped maintain the temperature and circulation, we discovered that having someone visit with me to take my mind off the dressing changes seemed to have a positive effect. The temperature drop would be less severe.

The swelling in my arms reached the point that the doctors had to make incisions to prevent my skin from tearing. They also had to add skin grafts. When my arms had gotten caught in the power take-off shaft, a lot of the skin had been shredded. My arms looked more like raw meat than human limbs.

It was a long time before I actually saw the skin on my arms after they had been reattached. Mercifully, the nurses also gave me medication before they did the dressing changes. If I had seen how bad my arms looked, it would have been extremely distressing. Once the grafting began, my arms resembled raw cube steak.

The grafts were obtained from my legs and backside. They shaved off patches of skin with an instrument that resembled a cheese slicer. Initially, they started harvesting skin from my thighs. Later, when they ran out of skin there, they took it from my butt. I wasn't happy about that at all. The harvested areas were now open sores that were covered with special dressings that reminded me of plastic food wrap with glue on one side. As the harvested areas on my legs started to heal, the itching and burning was unbearable.

The nurses were able to give me medication that made me as comfortable as possible. It didn't completely alleviate my discomfort, but I doubt I would have retained any sanity without it. At one point, however, my mother was convinced I had either completely lost my mind or I'd become brain damaged.

She came into my room in the ICU and noticed I was staring intently at the ceiling.

"What are you looking at?" she asked.

"I'm just watching all those cool fish swimming around," I replied.

The combination of drugs had provided me with this wonderful vision. I didn't know it was a hallucination. Of course, my mother was quite disturbed by what I said. She briefly thought I might be losing my mind. She immediately went for a doctor. The dosage of my medication was adjusted, and I didn't see any more fish.

Six days after the accident, my doctors and my parents held a news conference to update the public on my progress. There was so much interest in my story, and so much misinformation, that everyone felt it would be best to hold a news conference and present the official version. I wanted to participate, but Dr. Van Beek said it would be at least a couple of weeks before I could tolerate sitting in a wheelchair. I was still in serious condition and was battling an infection.

My parents were nervous about appearing before the media. This was all new to them, and my mother was a wreck. She has never forgotten how supportive Dr. Muldowney was.

"It was the first time I'd left John's side since I got to the hospital," she recalls. "Dr. Muldowney really helped. Still, I almost lost it when one journalist asked if John had carried his arms up to the house after the accident."

The doctors were able to tell the public that my arms were doing well and they were confident I'd overcome the infection. They explained the surgical procedure and told the media that my arms had been shortened approximately two and one-half inches to make connecting blood vessels and nerves easier. In short, the fact that I was young and healthy at the time of the accident meant there were a lot of reasons to be optimistic.

My parents thanked everyone for the cards, letters and donations, and my mom bragged up my nurses.

"John wants everyone to know he's going to make sure his nurses all get pay raises," mom told the media.

As I started to improve, I got to know some of the other patients in the ICU. There was a boy named Jason who had suffered a brain hemorrhage. His parents and mine became good friends while we were there. Jason gave me a poster of a nurse in a bikini that all the nurses signed for me. When Jason was able, he came to my room to visit. It was good to have someone my age to talk to.

The hospital staff began to prepare me for my transfer to another unit. I was anxious about leaving the ICU. I had gotten to know my nurses and they were almost like family.

Before my transfer, two of the nurses from the unit I would be transferred to came to visit me. Their names were Chuck and Lori and they wanted to become acquainted so I wouldn't feel like I was going to be with complete strangers. I was still anxious about being moved, but when the day for my transfer arrived it was much easier than I'd anticipated.

On January 23rd I was moved to 7-West where I had a primary nurse assigned to me. This meant I had one nurse to myself. This also meant there was a nurse with me almost continuously. It was good for my parents, too. They had more time for themselves so they started going out more, and they could get some rest.

The hospital also had a special footboard constructed for me while

I was on 7-West. It had controls that permitted me to use the call-light, turn on the television and room lights, or change channels with my feet. This gave me more independence and made it easier on my caretakers.

My ICU nurses would often stop to visit me before or after their shifts, or when they were on breaks. It was reassuring to see them.

After I was transferred to 7-West, more of my family came to visit. I don't remember all of their visits, but I do remember that we had a lot of fun on that unit. I also ate a lot of hamburgers and milkshakes. The hospital figured anything that increased my calorie intake gave my body the extra fuel it needed for healing.

Considering how bad my room smelled, I'm surprised anyone wanted to visit. I still had to contend with the skin grafts and the wounds on my arms. They would ooze and bleed. The stench of the drainage was overpowering. It made my caretakers and me nauseous. To improve the air quality, the nurses decorated my room with those Christmas tree air fresheners you can buy for your car. They also found a liquid deodorizer they could dump on me. It helped some, but when I was homesick it seemed like nothing eliminated the odor. I'll never forget that smell.

My dressings would reach the point where they were falling off and would have to be changed. Removing the dressings from my arms would still cause them to lose heat.

When they changed the dressings on my legs, the scabs that had started to form would peel off as the old dressings were removed. In addition, I was allergic to ordinary tape and paper tape. It irritated my skin, so they had to use silk tape. For a long time, I felt like an itching, stinking, oozing mess.

Things were tense, but I would joke around with my family and the nurses to take the pressure off. It took the staff a while to figure out when I was serious and when I wasn't. I even made one of the nurses cry. Her name was Patty, and I gave her a really hard time about her blonde hair. It took her awhile to realize that my blonde jokes were all in fun. After all, I'm blonde so I didn't think she'd take it personally.

When she finally realized I was joking, she started dishing it back. I gave her some nicknames like "Peppermint Patty" and "Dumb Blonde" and she bought me a dumb blonde t-shirt with 20 different dumb blonde jokes printed on it. I still wear that shirt and people still laugh at the jokes.

Besides my family, I got a lot of other visitors while I was on 7-West. Interest was fueled by ongoing news accounts and feature articles. For instance, the February 3, 1992 issue of *People Magazine* ran an article describing my ordeal entitled, "Too Tough to Die." At the request of North Dakota Senator Kent Conrad, the article was entered into the Congressional Record of the United States when the Senate was debating the rural health care issue.

Because of such publicity, I had celebrities who took the time to visit me. Several of the Minnesota Vikings football players came to the hospital. I was expecting them to be big, bulky guys. I blurted out the first thing that came to my mind when I saw them, which was, "You guys sure are small to be football players." They didn't hold it against me, and they presented me with a football signed by the entire team.

I'm sure most teenage boys would find the visit from the Viking cheerleaders equally exciting. They wore their uniforms and did a cheer for me.

There were other celebrities who sent wishes for my recovery. Bette Midler sent a huge flower arrangement that was indescribably beautiful. I got stuff from Whitney Houston, autographed compact discs from the group Firehouse, an autographed poster and some other things from Motley Crue. A lot of famous people in the music business sent me memorabilia.

It was terrific. I love music and I loved to sing. It had always been my dream to be a professional singer, so I was very touched that these great musicians were wishing me well.

Equally touching was the support I received from individuals. War veterans sent me their medals as a tribute to my "bravery." It was overwhelming, and I felt very honored.

Children seemed especially concerned. Some sent me personal items that were important to them. They felt it would give me some comfort and security. One little boy shoveled snow and sent me the five dollars he earned. One girl sent her pencil box. Some children sent their allowance money. Another girl sent her "tooth fairy" money and a card with the advice that "we should look at the things we can do." It was especially meaningful because she had spina bifida. It meant a lot to my family and me to know that people cared so much.

Contributions also poured in to the John Thompson Fund at the First State Bank of Goodrich. Within the first three weeks over 10,000 contributors had sent donations and expressions of concern to the bank. The last week in January, contributions came in at a rate of 1,000 per day. One person actually sent a $10,000 personal check. Some contributors also sent money directly to North Memorial Hospital.

Even though we had medical insurance at the time, there were a significant number of expenses that were not covered. The future would also hold a lot of unforeseen expenses. The financial help was greatly appreciated, and significantly reduced my concern that my family would go into bankruptcy because of my accident.

Our family was also offered a free trip to Disney World before I was released from the hospital. Sometime after that, I was asked if I would testify before Congress later that spring. They wanted my perspective on rural health care and emergency services. The two things would have overlapped.

Unfortunately, I made the innocent mistake of mentioning that my family and I were too busy to go to Washington, and that we had a schedule conflict because we were trying to plan a trip to Disney World. The media found out, and wrote that I was more interested in going to Disney World than testifying before Congress. That's not really how it was. It wasn't practical for me to testify before Congress because of my health and school concerns. We weren't able to schedule the trip to Disney World either.

Because of all the media and celebrity attention focused on me and the hospital, I met my first public relations director while I was on 7-West. His name was Jay and he was a North Memorial employee.

Considering that I wasn't very impressed by him at our first meeting, it's amazing that we became close friends. To me, he seemed very "preppy" and I thought he was "sucking up." Jay's manner was stiff and formal. I wasn't used to being around people in suits, and I wasn't used to being treated like I was so important. I realize he was maintaining a professional wall. I just wasn't prepared to deal with it.

I'm sure I must have told other hospital staff that I thought Jay was "too tightly wound." Thankfully, we got to know each other better. His wall came down a little, but I still teased him about being too tightly wrapped.

When I first met him, Jay was in his early twenties. He was more than a little green. Coming straight off the farm, I sure wasn't very polished. So we learned a lot together.

Jay would come to my room every day. He'd tell me what sorts of things had come for me in the mail. He'd let me know if there was any media interest, or if any celebrities wanted to meet me. He'd arrange all the details for the visits and accompany them to my room. Of course, if it was someone he wanted to meet, he'd present a convincing argument about why I wanted to meet them.

For instance, my very first meeting with Jay took place when he came to my room to discuss a possible visit by Emilio Estevez. I didn't recognize the name so I couldn't figure out who Emilio Estevez was. The son of actor Charlie Sheen, Emilio was in the Twin Cities shooting a "Mighty Ducks" movie.

At first, I wasn't very excited about meeting Emilio. My sister and the nurses thought I it was a great idea, and of course so did Jay. I agreed to the visit.

As soon as Emilio entered my room I recognized him. It was a terrific visit. He was very relaxed and friendly. I joked that when they made a movie about me, he could play the part.

"It would take a lot of make-up to make me look eighteen," he said.

Emilio gave me his director's chair and autographed some of his videos for me. He also gave me his phone numbers and addresses and we kept in touch for a while.

Jay served as a good filter. He had a feel for which visits would be beneficial for me. He also did a good job of coordinating the media and arranging interviews. It was a big deal to get the reporters and celebrities in and out of the hospital without causing a lot of disruption to the patients and staff. They'd have to sneak the stars in and out, and Jay got very adept at covert operations.

Over time, I realized Jay was sincerely concerned about what was going on in my life. I wasn't just some work assignment to him. I looked forward to his visits because I could talk to him as a friend rather than a doctor or family member. I frequently shared what I was feeling with Jay because I didn't want to bother my family. He'd come over the lunch hour, and feed me while we talked. It was definitely the medicine I needed.

I didn't want my family to know how truly afraid I was about the future. They were scared, too, and they felt responsible for my accident. I didn't want to add to their anxiety or their guilt. Jay let me express my fears and offered objective support.

Homesickness was a another problem. I missed my friends and the farm. I especially missed Tuffy. At home, when I needed someone to talk to, Tuffy filled the bill. Bringing Tuffy to the hospital had been discussed, but it was decided it was too much of an infection risk for me to see him. So, Jay substituted for my best friend.

Jay had a real public relations challenge with me at the hospital. He could have decided to handle it clinically or impersonally, but he showed a lot of heart. His expertise and assistance proved to be invaluable in the weeks and months ahead. Whenever I returned to North Memorial for follow-up care, we got a chance to visit and catch up.

Jay no longer works at North Memorial. He's moved on to another position but he's still always made time for me. He's become my personal public relations consultant, doing it as a favor. A lot of times when I'm in the cities I stay with him.

Chapter 4
Recovery

Lying in bed those first few weeks, I lost most of my muscle tone and my joints got very stiff. The staff on 7-west had the task of getting me on my feet and building up my strength. It was quite a job.

When you're forced to stay on your back for a long period of time, your equilibrium is affected. By the time I attempted sitting for the first time, I had been in a supine position for nearly three weeks. My head had been slightly elevated, but it wasn't the same as sitting completely upright. Everything was complicated by the fact that I was unable to use my arms to balance, and I was on medication. I didn't realize I would have to learn how to sit and how to walk again.

My primary nurse, Lori, was in charge of my mobility training. She explained that we were going to start with sitting at the edge of the bed. I told her that I was afraid I was going to hurt my arms, or cause them to fall off if I stood up.

Lori was very sensitive and caring. She didn't tell me I was being silly. When I told her I was scared that my arms might fall off, she felt so bad for me that she started crying. She conferred with some of the other nurses about how to make the whole process easier, and they decided to talk with the doctor about ordering some medication to help with my anxiety. They also explained that my arms couldn't fall off because they were literally bolted onto my body.

The medication did its job and I calmed down.

Up I went... and back down again in short order.

The first time I sat up, I turned white and got so dizzy I nearly passed out. It took several attempts over as many days to get to the point where I could sit up without passing out or throwing up. As soon as I mastered that, it was time to take my first step.

In preparation for getting to my feet, the nurses strapped a special belt around me so they would have something to hold onto when they pulled me up, and in case I started to fall.

They got me to my feet. Instantly, I felt the bile rising in my throat. I tried to take a deep breath, but got sick anyway and had to lie back down. Even so, it was progress. It only took a couple of days and I was finally able to stand, but only with complete assistance.

My circulatory system wasn't ready for the change in body position. Having spent all that time on my back with my head slightly elevated, my blood vessels hadn't had to fight gravity. Now, when I stood up, all the blood drained from my upper body down to my legs. In medicine, they call it orthostatic hypotension because it causes your blood pressure to drop. As the blood drained into my legs, it would rush to the areas from which my skin grafts had been harvested. For some reason, this made them itch and burn terribly every time I stood up. My legs turned dark blue and they hurt like hell.

My first step involved a sobering amount of effort. The nurses had hold of me on either side. There was also a nurse ahead of me and one behind.

It went something like this:

"Okay, John. Ready on three. One, two, three."

The nurses all took a step.

I just sort of fell forward.

"This is going to be harder than I thought," I said. "I thought I was moving my feet, but they weren't going anywhere, were they?"

I hadn't walked since January 11th and it was as if I had forgotten how. I had to re-establish the connection between my feet and my brain. Finally, I got the signals coordinated. I took two steps, got sick, and sat down in a chair beside my bed. After a couple of minutes in the chair I was ready to go back to bed.

For the next couple of days, I didn't walk more than a couple of steps with assistance. Of course, nurses are very goal oriented. The chair became my goal and they would move it a little further away each day. Lori seemed to know my limits, so I trusted her. The chair was just far enough away that I didn't get sick or pass out. The nurses would help me walk to it. Then I'd sit down and rest. When I felt better, I'd have to walk back to the bed.

It was painfully slow going, but with patience and pain medication I made it to the hall, then back to bed. The first time I made it the 50 feet to the nurses' station, everybody was so thrilled that they clapped and cheered for me. It was a little too exciting. I needed a wheelchair for the last half of the return trip.

Eventually, I was able to do the round trip to the nurses' station. Before long, I went the entire length of the hall, and then a trip around the whole floor. I was working towards my personal goal of paying a visit to my nurses in the Intensive Care Unit. When the day came that I walked down to ICU, I think they were more excited than I was. Aside from being happy to see me, they couldn't get over how tall I was. I looked smaller lying in my bed, and none of them had any idea that I would tower over them.

As hard as regaining my mobility was, I never considered giving up. I felt the only thing limiting me was going to be myself. I confess, fear was an obstacle. The future was uncertain, but the more I regained my strength, the less I worried about setbacks or hurting my arms. More than anything, I wanted to get well enough to return home to a "normal" life where I could spend time with my friends, family and dog.

The media and public interest in me continued to grow as I improved. Jay told me they had to get extra volunteers to help sort the huge volume of mail that kept pouring in from everywhere. Cards and letters continued coming at the rate of 1500 to 2000 per day. I even got a card from President Bush. The media had made me so well known, that in some cases mail made it through with only my name on the envelope and "USA" - no address needed.

Even with the extra help, there was a delay of several days in dispensing the mail. The hospital staff and volunteers did a great job of sending out thank you notes to people who sent gifts, flowers and monetary donations. It was a daunting task.

Based on my progress, Dr. Van Beek thought it was time to let the public see exactly how far I'd come. Jay made all the arrangements for my first public appearance. He even screened a hair stylist who'd volunteered to cut my hair. I was in desperate need of a trim and Ron did a great job of making me look presentable given what he had to work with.

The big day was scheduled for Thursday, February 6th, just 26 days after my arms had been traumatically amputated.

It was a hectic morning. It started with an exclusive television interview on *Good Morning America* with host Joan Lunden. I had to get up at 5:30 in the morning to do the program, which aired at 7:50 a.m. Eastern Standard Time. That was 6:50 a.m. in our time zone.

Dr. Van Beek was at my side for the interview, which I did from my wheelchair. It started with Ms. Lunden asking me about the day of the accident. She wanted to know who I called first for help. I told her about Tammy and Aunt Renae.

"By the time they got there, I'm told that you were hunched over in your bathtub. Why did you go there?"

"Well, I didn't want to get the carpets full of blood," I answered, almost sheepishly.

"So you were really thinking," Ms. Lunden said.

After that Dr. Van Beek explained how the care I received at the Harvey hospital had been crucial to saving my arms and to saving my life. When I first got to the hospital my systolic blood pressure was 60 and I was in shock. Dr. Van Beek credited Dr. Nyhus with giving me excellent care. By the time I was transferred to North Memorial I was no longer in shock.

Dr. Van Beek also explained the surgical procedure, which involved two teams of surgeons working on my arms simultaneously. He noted that time was an important factor in making the surgery a success.

"In a case like this we have twelve to eighteen hours to restore circulation to the lost parts, otherwise too much damage is done," he said.

"Do you have any feeling in your arms yet, or movement?" Ms. Lunden wanted to know.

"I have a lot of movement, but no feeling in my arms," I replied.

Ms. Lunden then asked about my prognosis and Dr. Van Beek concluded the interview by explaining that in my case he hoped to restore some pinching ability and grasp. He also said he hoped there would be restoration of some feeling so I could touch objects and tell what they were.

The *Good Morning America* interview was just the warm-up for the press conference that followed that afternoon. I had a few hours to rest before facing the full press at 4:00 p.m. That was just enough time to start thinking about it and to get nervous.

Before the afternoon conference I was given a dose of medication for pain and anxiety. I don't want to give the impression that I couldn't do anything unless I was doped up. It's standard procedure to give medication to someone who has sustained traumatic injury prior to activities involving stress or exertion. On the other hand, when I look back on that day, I realize I wasn't thinking at full capacity because there were a few things I forgot to tell the press.

I went down to the North Memorial auditorium in my wheelchair, which had a special tray. My arms rested on pillows on the tray. Lori wheeled me down. We were accompanied by Dr. Van Beek, my parents, Jay and a ring of security guards surrounding us.

When we got to the room I saw about five press people standing around and I started to get nervous. We got in a little further and there were another fifteen reporters and photographers standing around. It was really intimidating once we got up to the front of the room. I couldn't count all the media people. I was told there were over one hundred.

Reporters for newspapers, radio, magazines and television — they were all there along with the brightest and hottest lights I'd ever seen. Lori positioned my wheelchair at a table in the front of the room. People started bringing up tape recorders and pinning microphones on me. It was disorienting but I kept my nerve and tried to smile. Looking back at the tapes, I can see that I had that "deer in the headlights" look. I'd lost over 30 pounds since the accident, and I looked like a little kid rather than a high school senior.

Dr. Van Beek sat to my left and made an opening statement expressing that he and the other doctors were confident the circulation in my arms was stable.

"At this point in time," he said, "the most important thing to be determined is how well the nerves that were repaired in John's arms will regenerate and repair themselves."

He explained that nerve tissue can repair itself at a rate of one-half to one inch per month.

"John's nerves were repaired at the level of his shoulders," he continued. "Since they must grow from there to his forearm and hand, it will be some time, and there will be additional surgeries before we can determine how much use he will have of his hands."

Dr. Van Beek told the reporters there would be one more surgery before I was released. I looked on, trying to keep my heart out of my throat as he told the world, "In the very best of recoveries, he will have a significant handicap that will affect the way he does things for the rest of his life. My goal as his surgeon is to provide him with the ability to pinch, grasp, and touch and feel objects."

Again Dr. Van Beek commended the health care personnel who had worked to save my life and my arms. As soon as he opened things up for questions, the press wanted to revisit the day of the accident.

"Can you tell us a little bit about that day? What was running through your mind that day as you were out there with the farm machinery?"

"It was just another day unloading the truck," I said.

"And then the accident happened. What were you thinking then?"

"I knew I had to get to the house, and get an ambulance out there right away before I bled to death."

"You don't seem to think that what you've done is particularly courageous and everyone else does," said another reporter.

"I don't," I answered.

"Can you try to put us in your place?"

"I think they've really blown things out of proportion... I think everybody could have done the same thing."

"How did you keep your composure?" someone asked.

"What do you mean?" I said bewildered by the question.

"How did you not freak out?"

"Well, I did at first when I noticed my arms were gone," I answered with a grin.

The crowd gave a little laugh and I relaxed a bit. The press asked me about my plans for going home and gave me a chance to say "hi" to my relatives and friends back in North Dakota.

"I'll be home in about two more weeks," I informed them.

"Why did you wait in the bathroom?" someone wanted to know.

"My mom hates me when I say this," I prefaced my answer, "but I didn't want to get the carpets full of blood."

My poor mother didn't want the world to have the mistaken impression that she thought her carpets were more important than her son.

"Can you explain why you were thinking about that at a time like this?" the reporter pressed for more information.

"I don't know... I'm just a clean person," I answered and again there were chuckles from the crowd.

"Were you afraid for your life?"

"Yeah, at first. But then my aunt got there and that helped a lot."

The reporters asked about the outpouring of support from around the world and what it meant to me.

"Thanks a lot," I said. "It really means a lot to me."

"How do you feel looking forward?" someone asked.

"It's scary," I answered. "I don't know how much use I'll have of my arms. There are things I won't be able to do now and big changes I'll have to make in my life."

No one really had any idea how much my arms would improve. There simply weren't enough cases like mine to give any basis for predicting an outcome.

"What can you feel now from your shoulders down?" came the

big question.

To demonstrate, I waved to the crowd with my left arm and everyone clapped. Then I gave a little shrug of my right shoulder. There were splints on both of my arms, so the movement was restricted. I explained that I could feel things at the level of my shoulders. I told the crowd my right side was more painful because it had more breaks than the left.

By the end of the news conference I was exhausted. Being nervous, coupled with the heat from the lights, I was soaked with sweat. Frankly, I looked like hell.

Until later, when I had a chance to see a tape of the news conference, it didn't hit me that I left some very important details out of my description of the day of the accident. When the reporter asked me how I kept from freaking out, I should have given credit to my best friend. If Tuffy hadn't been beside me, I never would have recovered my composure enough to make it to the house.

Chapter 5
Tuffy

Tuffy was my dog from the start. I was ten years old and he was around six weeks old when we first met.

My dad had taken me along to a Saturday livestock sale in Herreid, South Dakota. It was autumn, and I considered it a treat to go. Besides the cattle, pigs, or sheep, sometimes there were companion animals for sale, too. There was a family that had a box full of Blue Heeler puppies and they wanted seventy-five dollars per puppy.

Times were tough for farmers, so seventy-five dollars for a puppy was extravagant. I looked the puppies over. There was one that seemed to have a special gleam in his eye. He licked my hand and seemed to thoroughly enjoy it when I held him. I casually wandered back to my dad waiting for the right moment to pop the question.

"Dad, can I buy that puppy?" I asked.

Of course, I didn't have seventy-five dollars of my own. Dad pulled a ten spot out of his pocket.

"If they'll let you have him for this, you can take him home," he said as he handed me the money.

I marched over with the ten dollar bill and turned on the charm.

"These are really nice puppies," I said. "I think this little one likes me."

Tuffy was licking my hand.

"I'd sure like to give him a good home, but I've only got ten dollars here. Do you think you could let me have him for that?"

It worked. They accepted the ten dollars and I carried my new best friend back to my dad. Dad was surprised they let me have him for only ten dollars.

On the ride home, as I held him in my arms, I couldn't help noticing he was a compact ball of muscles. That's how he got his name.

Tuffy seemed to take to our farm right away. He loved the outdoors, and we had plenty of wide open spaces for him to enjoy.

When Tuffy first came to live with us, I made a bed for him in the garage, but as he grew up I thought he should have his own house. Dad let me convert an old tool shed into a doghouse for him. I insulated the walls with styrofoam to keep it warm in the winter. Then, I nailed paneling over the styrofoam.

I probably spent as much time in the doghouse as Tuffy did. In the winter I camped in there with him so he wouldn't get lonely. It was pretty snug. The insulation did its job, and we stayed warm even when it was sub-zero weather.

Tuffy was a great dog for kids. He was patient and gentle. He was also very protective. If someone appeared to threaten one of us, he wasted no time letting them know that was a bad idea. He only had a few bad habits. For instance he liked to chew on feet and nibble on toes, something he didn't do aggressively. It was just one way he could get our attention.

One of Tuffy's favorite games involved pulling us around by our pants. If there was someplace he wanted you to go, he'd grab a pants leg and start to tug. Most of the time, he did it just for fun. It was exciting on ice. He'd pull, and we'd slide along trying to keep our balance. We got a thrill out of our "sled" dog.

Wrestling with us kids was another of Tuffy's favorite past times. He was very careful and never tried to hurt anyone. In fact, he'd actually look and act ashamed if he thought he accidentally hurt you.

Tuffy was friendly to the whole family, but he was an outdoor dog and didn't even seem to want to come in the house. He was also definitely my dog. I got very used to him being my shadow as soon as I stepped out the door. I talked to him so much I think he understood English better than a lot of people.

As the youngest child in a farm family, I didn't have a lot of friends to play with. I sure didn't have an opportunity to make a lot of friends in my grade school. So, Tuffy filled a big void. It was simply impossible to look into those big brown eyes and feel lonesome. Tuffy taught me what it meant to have a best friend.

Like a lot of farm dogs, Tuffy worked for a living. He was a natural herder, which was great since I enjoyed working around the live-stock, and we needed a good herd dog. He could herd cows and pigs with the best of them. He also loved to ride. We'd go for rides on the motor-cycle and the four-wheeler, or he'd jump in the pickup. Riding was the only thing better than running as far as Tuffy was concerned. It was a great way for both of us to escape.

There are some people who don't believe dogs can "think" or "feel." They believe every action or expression of affection an animal shows is some sort of conditioned response. But Tuffy had a way of looking inside me. He could tell when I was feeling down and he'd make sure he was close by. He wasn't just sensitive to me, he was concerned about the rest of the family as well. He always seemed to have his radar on. If something was wrong, if someone was sick, or worried, Tuffy sensed it and seemed ready to listen. Sometimes I'd sit in the yard or on the deck, and he'd lay his big head on my lap. He'd look up at me and his eyes would speak volumes.

Chapter 6
Homecoming

The day after the news conference, a tutor came to the hospital to see me for the first time. My school in Bowdon had already told my parents I could graduate with my class later in the spring, but Dr. Van Beek didn't want me to fall behind. He arranged for a tutor to help with my studies for the remainder of my hospital stay.

It was probably a waste of time. I was scheduled for another surgery before my release, and I was still on a significant amount of medication. There were simply too many distractions for me to concentrate on schoolwork. The tutor would come, and we would talk. I didn't learn much.

A man named Jerry also contacted me about a personal computer. He worked at Business Machines and Sales. The company wanted to give me a computer that was loaded with a special voice recognition program called Dragon. It made it possible for me to write letters, something I'm now able to do with my hands. I simply spoke into a microphone and the computer spelled out whatever I said. Jerry came to the hospital several times to teach me how to use it and to make the adjustments necessary to get the thing to work. It was great.

The last two weeks of my hospital stay flew by. After the remaining surgery, which involved more skin grafts, recovery went more quickly than expected. There was a lot to do to prepare me for my return home. I wasn't going to have round the clock nursing care once I got back to Hurdsfield. There would be home health nurses helping with bathing and dressing changes every morning, but for the rest of the day I'd either have to do things for myself or have my family help me.

The hospital wasn't sending a security detail home with me either. As long as I was a patient at North Memorial, I was in a very protected environment. My parents never thought they'd see the day when we'd need security at the farm. Until my accident they'd never even locked the house when they left home. After the accident there was a steady stream of people who found their way to our place. Some were reporters, and some were just curious. Most of them were more polite than the strangers at the hospital, but we didn't want to have our privacy totally invaded. My parents decided it was time to invest in more locks for the house and the outbuildings.

To prepare for my homecoming, my mother returned to Hurdsfield a couple of days before my discharge. My cousin Tim picked her up at the hospital and drove her home. She had to make appointments, set up the home care, and get the house in order. The school also asked if they could hold a big "welcome home" pep rally, and of course the press was interested in covering my arrival.

My family also had to figure out some way to transport all the gifts that had been sent to the hospital. When family members and friends from North Dakota came to visit, my parents made sure their cars, vans or pickups were packed with stuff for the return trip. Even so, there was still enough left at the hospital that my brother had to bring his semi truck and trailer down after I was discharged and pack the rest of it.

Dr. Van Beek wouldn't allow me to travel home by car. He gave me a choice. I could take a commercial flight on Northwest Airlines or fly home in the hospital's helicopter. No offense to Northwest Airlines, which was kind enough to donate the airfare for my trip home, but I voted for the helicopter.

Discharge day arrived on Tuesday, February 25th, six weeks after my accident. The nurses got me bathed and dressed before the wheelchair ride to the helicopter garage. My dad was there for all of the last minute instructions. I think he was happy we were going home, but nervous at the same time.

Jay made all the arrangements for a farewell press conference. My discharge was big news and the press wanted to cover my departure from North Memorial as well as my arrival home. A lot of people from around the world had been praying and hoping for my recovery. It seemed important to let them share the day. Their support had been a big boost and I wanted them to see how far I'd come.

Lori got me into a wheelchair for the ride to the heli-port. When I got to the door leading to the heli-port, I stepped out of the wheelchair and walked into the garage. Once inside the garage I hesitated. I wasn't prepared for such a send-off. People were applauding and there were reporters everywhere. They had to clear a path for me to get to the podium. There were so many people I couldn't even see where to go.

"How does it feel to be going home?" came the first question.

I couldn't resist.

"Well, I came down in three pieces, and I'm going home in one."

For a second there was silence and everyone stared at me blankly. People just weren't sure how to react. Then there was a chuckle somewhere in the room and laughter started to spread.

I gave everyone a wave, then told them that I was scared to be going home. I appreciated all the assistance the hospital staff and volunteers had given me and my family, and would I really miss it when I returned to Hurdsfield. I think my parents were even more anxious about going home than I was.

The kindness and consideration our family had been shown while I was in Robbinsdale amazed both my mom and dad. People in our hometown had pitched in to help with the farm while we were away, but even people who didn't know us had been extremely kind and generous. It amazed us that there was such an outpouring of support from people in the Robbinsdale and Minneapolis area.

Going home was going to be a big adjustment for all of us. We were confident we could pull together with our community and get through the challenges in the weeks, months and years to come, but we also felt things were happening too fast. At discharge, I had sensation down to the level of my elbows. We didn't know how much more improvement there would be, but we hoped I'd continue to gain both strength and feeling in my arms.

Personally, I was anxious about mom having to care for me and wrap my arms. She'd only gotten one chance to learn how to remove my dressings, apply the xeroform, and rewrap my wounds. This was part of the daily routine because I was now taking showers every day. I still had open sores where the skin grafts were harvested, and there was drainage from the grafted areas on my arms. I was unable to feed, dress or bathe myself. There would be a lot to contend with, especially without the assistance we were used to from nurses, doctors and therapists. Ahead, we'd find out there simply was no way to be completely prepared.

When it was time to leave, I said one last goodbye to my nurses. They all came for the send-off. I had a hard time leaving them, especially Lori. She had seen me through some very emotional times. She had given me the encouragement and motivation to get out of my bed, back on my feet, and walking again. When she hugged me, I didn't want to let go. I was crying and said, "I just feel like I'm going to die."

"It's going to be all right, you're not going to die," she said reassuringly.

She was right.

The flight team loaded me onto the helicopter and the helicopter was pushed out of the garage. The pilot started the engine, and I had time for a last wave goodbye before we lifted off at 11:00 a.m.

I would be back for additional surgeries. The total would come to 15 in the first 18 months after the initial surgery to reattach my arms. But physically, the worst was over.

There was a sunny blue sky, making it a great day to fly. I was excited about going home but I was also scared to death. I was losing my security blanket and my future held a lot of uncertainty.

Once in the air, the helicopter pilot flew low enough over the hospital that I could see everything. In spite of my anxiety, it was liberating to be outside after six weeks in North Memorial. I sat up so I could see what was going on for a good part of the trip.

My dad was with me on the flight home. The trip was a treat for him. He'd been in the Army's First Battalion 8th Cavalry Airborne and was part of a helicopter flight crew in Viet Nam in 1967. This was better. It was a state-of-the-art machine, and no one was shooting at him.

Back home, mom was scrambling to get everything ready for my homecoming. All of this was under the watchful eye of the press. She had consented to allow reporters to come to the house to cover my arrival. They were there hours before the actual event. Mick was in the yard grinding feed with the auger when mom suddenly noticed there was no noise coming from the barnyard and she got nervous about it. She gathered herself quickly, but it was one of those moments when a person wonders if anything will ever be the same. The press just happened to be around to witness it.

We arrived in Harvey and the helicopter touched down at St. Aloisius Hospital at 2:30 p.m. I could see people clapping and cheering before I got out of the helicopter. The hospital had a wheelchair ready for me, but I walked from the helicopter to the building. Everyone cheered even louder.

The crowd included my entire high school class, lots of friends and reporters. The fire department, police officers, and the volunteer ambulance squad were also there — and there were lots of "Welcome Home" banners and signs. It was great to be back, and this was a hero's welcome.

My mom and Mick met us at the hospital. Our regular physician, Dr. Charles Nyhus, performed a quick check-up. It was standard procedure to make sure I'd handled the flight and to ensure continuity of care. Then there was another press conference.

Someone asked what I was looking forward to.

"I'm looking forward to having some of my mom's chicken."

My mom laughed and looked embarrassed.

"I made roast beef for dinner. I'm sorry," she apologized.

Everyone was amazed at the range of motion I had in my arms. They called it miraculous, but there were a lot of things that had to happen to bring me to that point.

If it weren't for the rural ambulance volunteers, my arms and I probably wouldn't have made it to the hospital in Harvey. If Dr. Curt Nyhus and the staff at St. Aloisius hospital in Harvey hadn't known how to treat a traumatic injury like mine, it's unlikely I would have been stable enough to transport to a distant trauma center. If Doctor Knutson, hadn't remembered the replantation work being done at North Memorial, I never would have been sent there. If Dr. Van Beek and Dr. Muldowney hadn't had such skill in vascular and microsurgery, my arms would never have been reattached. Finally, without the care and attention I received from the staff and nurses at North Memorial, I would not have recovered as quickly as I did.

After the press conference, the helicopter was waiting to take me the 25 miles from Harvey back to our farm. My dad drove to the farm and Mick and my mom got to make the trip in the helicopter with me. When we reached Hurdsfield, the pilot circled the town a couple of times before heading east to the farm. Looking down from the helicopter, I could see hundreds of cars on the gravel road leading to our place. There were three or four state highway patrol officers keeping on-lookers away so the helicopter could land, and so we wouldn't be mobbed.

The pilot landed the helicopter in a field about a thousand feet away from the house, it was a safe distance just to make sure nothing went wrong and no one got hurt. My Grandma's car was parked near by, and my cousin Terry was waiting to drive Mick, mom and I from the helicopter to the house.

When we reached the front of the house, I got out of the car and walked toward the front steps. Here was my first serious obstacle. I'd gotten out of the hospital before any one had a chance to work with me on navigating stairs. With my limited sense of balance, this was a major problem. I had to have assistance. I didn't have the strength in my legs to push myself up on each step. Even with help, I reached the top step in a sitting position, instead of standing up. It was obvious that I was going to need more practice.

Once inside the house, our poodle Tinker was so happy to see me she wouldn't leave me alone. I walked into the dining room. Then I saw Tuffy sitting on the back deck waiting.

My folks helped me sit down on the floor by the patio door. Then they slid the patio door open and Tuffy rushed in. He was so gentle. He knew I'd been hurt and he didn't want to jump on me. He laid his head in my lap, so I could pet him. This was the first time Tuffy had ever been in the house. In fact, before my accident you couldn't force him to come inside. This time, he didn't care. He just wanted to be with me. It was one of those moments when nothing else mattered.

I sat there for quite a while petting Tuffy. A photographer was taking pictures of our reunion but I didn't even notice him. This was the dog that had saved my life and nothing was going to come between us at this moment in time.

Chapter 7
Life resumes

That first day home was exhausting. After I'd gotten settled at the farm, I did another exclusive interview, this one with reporter Asha Blake from KARE 11 TV News out of Minneapolis-St. Paul. It was a "How does it feel to be home?" interview. Frankly, I don't remember a lot about it. But Asha became a friend of our family. She came to visit the farm several times.

After the interview with Asha, I went to bed for a nap. When I woke up, a couple of hours later, there were still some neighbors and news people at the house. I spent a little time visiting with them, and then ate the roast beef dinner my mother had prepared. That was all I could handle.

I was completely exhausted and started to wonder if I should have stayed longer at North Memorial. In fact, my whole family had reservations about my early discharge. The North Memorial staff felt I'd recover more quickly at home, but there had been so little time to prepare.

In retrospect, my homecoming was just a prelude. Over the next couple of years my life would become increasingly frenzied. There simply would never be enough time to adjust. But I had no way of knowing that on my first night back at the farm.

The next morning, the home health nurses arrived at the house. It was an enormous help. I didn't want to put my parents in the position of having to do everything for me. It wouldn't have been good for them, and it certainly wouldn't have been good for me. I think they would have tried to do too much. The nurses, with the advantage of professional training, had a better feel for how much I should attempt — and how fast. That doesn't mean I always listened.

The first case in point was driving.

What is more natural than a teen-age boy, wanting to get behind the wheel? My car was my freedom and I was already itching to see if I could drive. My mother was altogether against the idea. In fact, I think she was secretly hoping I wouldn't drive again until I was in my thirties.

Anyway, after the nurses were gone, I said I wanted to go outside. I headed straight for my Oldsmobile. I thought I'd start with my old car rather than my new Honda.

After a lot of fumbling, I got the key in the ignition, and managed to turn it. Nothing. The battery was dead.

I'd have to try the Honda. The problem was that the Oldsmobile was an automatic and the Honda was a stick shift.

I managed to get the Honda started and with a lot of effort even got it shifted into gear, but I still couldn't go anywhere. The emergency brake was set and I didn't have the dexterity to get it off. My mother refused to release it for me, so I didn't do any driving that day. It was probably just as well. I didn't want to wreck my Honda since I'd just gotten it, and I didn't want to wreck the Olds Cutlass Supreme since it was for sale.

The first week at home, I spent a lot of time learning and figuring out how to do things for myself. Even sleeping required adjustment. My bed at home was hard and flat. I'd gotten used to having my head and legs elevated at the hospital, so it was difficult to get comfortable.

Going to the bathroom was one of the worst adjustments. I wouldn't let my mother take me. We experimented with a couple of ideas trying to make me independent in this area. We even rigged a stick wrapped with toilet paper as a sort of self-cleaner. It was mounted to the wall, and didn't work worth a crap, so to speak. Fortunately, a company that makes a special toilet seat came to my rescue within only a few days of my homecoming. The seat is called a "Toto." It's kind of like a bidet. It washes and dries your bottom, and I still use one in my home. Frankly, it's a lot more hygienic than toilet paper and I'm surprised it hasn't caught on for common use in the home.

Getting dressed by myself was a challenge, too. Fastening buttons without the full use of my hands was impossible. I learned to appreciate slip-on loafers even more than cowboy boots.

The first week I was home we tried to work out my schedule for returning to school. I returned to Bowdon High the following week, but I would never have a full schedule of classes.

My first day back, the school greeted me with a big party and pep rally. My classmates had painted a big banner that said, "WELCOME BACK, JOHN ITM." Few people knew the letters "ITM" stood for a song I was fond of parodying. If the school administration had known the song was, "I Touch Myself" they would have insisted the letters weren't on the banner. The cheerleaders did cheers, and there was a special song composed by one of the teachers. The ever-present press was also there. School was where I first began to feel the press was an intrusion, but at this point I still didn't know how much of an intrusion.

During the pep rally I was seated at a table in the center of the gym with the rest of my high school class. The school also served cake and ice cream. Since I couldn't feed myself, I didn't have any. I felt it was too degrading to be fed like a baby in front of my classmates.

I didn't attend class that first day. I was wishing I had. I didn't want to be different, and this seemed like one more thing that made me different from everyone else.

After the party, my mom drove me to Harvey for therapy. This would be a major part of my routine in the months to come. To regain as much function as possible, I was going to Harvey for therapy for three to four days per week.

Looking back, I was so busy regaining my physical strength that I had very little time for actual schoolwork. Sure, I wanted to graduate with the rest of my class in May. But, I just couldn't devote the energy or time to school those last few months. It was a very difficult time.

I worried a lot about fitting in at school. Everyone was trying so hard to be helpful, but they were also slightly afraid. People would give me a wide berth because they were afraid to touch me for fear of hurting me. It made me feel as though there was a huge separation. I'd been used to friendly physical contact before my accident. A slap on the back, a pat on the shoulder, a slug in the arm — of course, no one wanted to do that anymore. But there was no physical contact at all.

One day, I'd had enough. I wanted my classmates to know that I wasn't going to break. I purposely bumped into one of my classmates, Heather.

"I'm so sorry," she started apologizing. "Did I hurt you. Oh, I'm sorry, I'm sorry. Are you all right?"

She was really shaken and couldn't quit apologizing.

"I'm fine. I ran into you on purpose," I said.

Heather kept apologizing.

Everyone was like that. I wasn't sure if they were afraid of hurting me, or if they were simply afraid of me. I wanted them to treat me like a normal person, but that was easier said than done.

Classes presented other challenges. Sometimes, it was comical. Even though I was extremely self-conscious, I couldn't help but see the humor in the situation.

My morning class was history. I was not an inspired student. It would have been a lot more interesting to me if we studied about the great wars and battles, but instead we focused more on government. Regardless, I thought our teacher was great. His name was Mr. Schlegel and he was also the school principal.

Whenever Mr. Schlegel scheduled a test, and we hadn't studied for it, we could distract him from the exam by getting him to talk about one of his favorite subjects — his pigs. By encouraging him to tell pig stories we could stall long enough to get him to postpone the test until the next day. Since I also raised pigs, we talked about pigs a lot in class. They really are intelligent animals. I thought Mr. Schlegel's pig stories were great — not just because they bought us time but because they were entertaining.

Mr. Schlegel had kept in close contact while I was at North Memorial. It was important to him that I graduate and he wanted to make sure I completed History and English, which were both required.

Mr. Schlegel always opened history class by discussing current world events. One of my first days back at school, we opened with the usual routine. Mr. Schlegel called on me.

"What's new?" he asked.

I paused for a moment to think, then started laughing. I had actually been a current event myself. The thought must have occurred to everyone because every student in the room started to laugh, too. Then Mr. Schlegel asked us to take out our history books and turn to a certain page.

My book was inside my desk under the lid. I got the lid open without much trouble. Using both fists, I managed to lift the book out of the desk and move it to the top. Then I had to open to the specified page that was in the middle of the book. The problem was that my hands and fingers still had no muscle tone. When I pushed objects with them, they just bent against the pressure.

I got the cover opened and started trying to turn the pages to the place I needed to be. Mr. Schlegel saw I was struggling.

"Do you need any help, John?" he asked.

I wasn't ready to admit defeat, and I didn't want people to get in the habit of doing things for me. I thought I'd make a lot more progress if I kept trying to do things for myself.

"No, I don't need any help," I answered.

I kept working at getting to the right page while the class was discussing the chapter. I was concentrating really hard. Finally, I got within a couple of pages of the right spot, but I just couldn't flip the last two pages over. Then I noticed how quiet it was in the room.

Looking up I saw the whole class staring at me. They were on the edges of their chairs waiting to see if I'd be able to get it. I just smiled. It was extremely embarrassing, but when my classmates laughed I found it was encouraging. They wanted me to be able to turn the pages just as much as I wanted to be able to do it.

"Let me keep trying," I told them.

When I finally arrived at the correct page, the whole class cheered for me. That was just as embarrassing but I was pleased I was able to do it on my own.

Already, I was aware of how the accident had changed my attitude about achieving things. It was a strange transformation. I never did more than the minimum needed to get by. Before the accident, when I had two good arms, I would have happily let someone else turn the pages of my book. Since then, I had come to the realization that I couldn't take any real pride in anything or feel any sense of achievement unless I did as much as I could for myself.

School, however, would remain one of my lowest priorities. With the physical demands of recovery and therapy, there was little chance I was going to turn into an outstanding student in the last few weeks of the semester. My memory of those weeks is hazy, but I think I only took one history test. I more or less showed up and talked about the chapter, and passed the class.

English wasn't a lot different. I wrote a few short stories and read some books. That was enough to pass the class.

I shouldn't have graduated. But no senior in my shoes would have said, "I think you should make me come back again next year."

Everyone was doing what they thought was best for me. Today, I can see it was a well-intentioned mistake. I wasn't ready to resume classes, but my teachers and classmates became invested in helping me graduate on schedule.

Admittedly, it was a huge distraction when I returned to school. Aside from my physical challenges, there were other problems to deal with. There were several attempts by the media to sneak into the building during class. Apparently, some reporters thought strange people with television cameras wouldn't be noticed in a school with only 56 total students.

In spite of returning to school, I missed a lot of the socialization. Because I was attending on such a limited basis, I didn't spend a lot of time there. When I was there over the lunch hour, I didn't go to the cafeteria because I couldn't feed myself. The only time I got to spend with my friends was while I was in class. It was a very isolating experience.

I started to dwell on the idea that I was a freak. I didn't know what I was going to do with the rest of my life, or even what I'd be able to do. While I was still at North Memorial I had begun to see that the public had their own perceptions of who I was. There were people who just wanted an opportunity to touch me because they believed they would be healed. It was strange and frightening. How could people feel so desperate and hopeless in their lives that they would believe I could provide them with a miracle?

My parents couldn't believe it either. At North Memorial, when people were asking to touch me, my mother made the comment, "Well, he's not Jesus Christ." We quickly learned that we had to be very careful about what we said and to whom we said it. After my mother's comment we received a number of critical phone calls and letters from people who thought it was inappropriate.

No doubt, the press reports contributed to the notion that I had some sort of miraculous powers. It was repeatedly broadcast that I had to have "superhuman strength" to survive my ordeal. Apparently, some people started to believe I was superhuman. They also believed they had a right to ask me to help them.

One woman called me from Florida. Her son had been shot in the shoulder and had some permanent damage. She wanted to fly the boy to North Dakota to meet me for lunch, then fly him home again. There were other people who made similar requests. Even if people didn't believe I could heal them, they expected a lot.

At North Memorial, Jay or the staff fielded most of the requests from the public. At home, we were on our own. My parents, and my mother in particular, filtered most of the requests. Some people took my refusals as personal insults. They thought I was ungrateful for my recovery and expected I should be more willing to share my experience. In fact, I had neither the strength nor the time to deal with most of the people who wanted to meet me — but few of them understood that.

We received disturbing letters, too. People were aware that I had received monetary gifts after the accident. There was no shortage of people who had ideas about how I should spend the money. Some of them were demanding. Some felt they had to express their belief that I wasn't being responsible. Without knowing whether we had donated money to a certain cause, there were those that criticized me for not giving money to different organizations. Sometimes we got solicitations from groups. If we said "no" they could become hostile.

Then there was the endless succession of reporters who wanted to cover my story. Some of them were courteous, but others totally disregarded our privacy. While this was going on, I was being advised that I should act a certain way to maintain my public image and popularity. It's easy to see how the situation could get out of control.

My family and I had never anticipated having to deal with "my public." We were just average country people from North Dakota. We weren't used to having to phrase our words carefully to safeguard a public image. The experience was mentally exhausting. In the first months after the accident I was already feeling a great deal of pressure and loss of identity.

I used one of the stories I wrote for English class to vent some of my feelings on paper. At the same time, I didn't want people to know how dark my view of the world was becoming. It wouldn't have been good for my "image." It was safer to cover my feelings with fiction.

The class assignment was to write a story from the perspective of someone who had been in a coma for twenty years, and then awakened. We were supposed to write about what we found when we woke up.

My story painted a picture of apocalyptic disaster. The sky was orange from nuclear fallout. World War III had erupted while I was in my fictitious coma. I wrote that it would have been better if I had died instead of awaking to this hell.

From 1992 to the 25th Century
by John Thompson

Dad and I were working cattle one day, when a steer charged me, and I got hit falling on a rock and striking my head. The steer kept hitting me so Dad had gotten the steer's attention so it would come after him instead of me and leave me alone. While the steer chased Dad, Mom got me out of the barn and took me to a safe place.

The paramedics arrived shortly after and took me to the hospital where I was in a coma for many years. They said I couldn't hear when people talked to me, but I could. They said I would not live with such a bad head injury. They said I would die very soon. I proved them wrong.

When I awoke it was many years later and many things had changed for the worse. The sky was red with acid and other pollutants in the air. The water was poisonous to drink, or to get on your skin. People wore heavy white suits to keep out the ultraviolet rays from the holes in the ozone layer. They all wore dark sunglasses to keep out dangerous rays.

When I awoke to this nightmare, I wished I would have died instead of waking up to this terrible world that I now live in. The doctors tried to get me to accept the new world but it was too awful.

I was still hooked up to machines, so I was going to unplug them and realized I could just take off my mask and breath the deadly air into my lungs and it would all be over. The air was very strong smelling and I died very quickly and painlessly. I hope I never wake up again.

In truth, those were my feelings. I felt pulled and stretched, but I didn't want people to know that I felt depressed — that my outlook was less than optimistic. In countless news stories, people had called my recovery a story of hope. How could I let all those people down? My parents had repeatedly said that it was my positive attitude that had pulled them through the ordeal. I didn't want to disappoint them, my caregivers, friends, and the numerous well wishers around the world.

My trips to physical therapy in Harvey were usually helpful because I could talk with the therapists and staff, but I recall one session when even that didn't work. There were reporters there asking me questions about the accident and my progress. It hit me that while everyone was interested in my story, very few people knew or even wanted to know what I was feeling. Now, instead of developing friendships, I was being observed like a rat in some experiment or a specimen on a slide. People wanted to see a happy face. They didn't want to hear that I was struggling. I broke down in front of the cameras. My therapist, Kelly, cleared the room.

"What's going on?" he asked.

"I just feel so tired," I said. "I don't know if I can deal with this any more."

The incident passed. Everyone chalked it up to being exhausted and having a bad day. But deep down I knew something was wrong. I couldn't identify exactly what the trouble was and I didn't know how to communicate it. But little cracks were forming in my emotional wall.

The spring music contest was another time when the cracks started to show. Usually, music contests were no big deal. They were nothing to get nervous over, but this time was different. The contest was held in Jamestown in April. When it was time for me to sing my solo, the auditorium was packed with people. All the other contestants, teachers and parents wanted to hear me sing.

The musical selection I performed was "I Believe." I got through the song, but stumbled over the first few words of the second verse. When I finished, the judge asked me to start over at the beginning. He advised me to take "a big breath" before I started. After the second time through, the judge came up and talked to me for a little bit. He was just trying to give me advice, but I felt totally humiliated. It was nerve wracking.

As the end of the school year approached there were a few highlights. My classmates talked me into attending the prom, something I hadn't planned to do. If I was going, I wanted to drive myself. It wasn't acceptable to have my date drive, and I certainly wasn't going to have one of my parents drive me.

I called Dr. Van Beek and explained that I wanted to find a car I could easily drive. He'd been pushing me to try as much as I could. I thought he'd support this idea and have some suggestions on adaptive equipment.

Dr. Van Beek's reaction wasn't what I'd expected

"Absolutely not," he said. "You shouldn't try driving. You don't have the mobility or the strength to drive a car. It's just too dangerous."

So much for professional advice. He should have known I wouldn't listen. Driving was freedom. If I could drive myself, it would also give my mother more free time. I had to rely on her to take me to school, to therapy, and anywhere I else I needed to go. I thought driving myself was reasonable.

I went car shopping. It was no easy task finding a suitable vehicle. I needed an automatic because I couldn't shift. I also needed one with push button controls because I couldn't turn knobs. There were only two models that met the specifications — the 1992 Chevy Lumina Z34 and the Olds Cutlass Supreme. I chose the Olds because the buttons were in the steering wheel. They were much easier to reach than the dash.

My dad rode with me when I made the test-drive. He was nervous. I'm sure he was thinking that even though the accident hadn't killed me, my driving might kill both of us. He remembered that I liked to drive fast, and I hadn't been behind the wheel for a long time. I'm sure he was thinking, "What's going to happen if John wrecks the car before we're out of the lot?"

The car was easy to drive and I liked it. The push buttons were simple to use, and I reasoned it would get even easier with practice.

The first time I drove the car after we bought it, I took it to school. My mother was with me. She wasn't ready to turn me loose on the road without supervision. To make her feel better, I let her ride along.

It was the usual route to school. There were never any cops on the stretch — but wouldn't you know it? I got nailed for speeding, even with my mom in the car. The officer said I was doing 78 miles per hour in a 55 zone. I couldn't believe I was going that fast. He also recognized me right away.

"Are you able to drive a car?" he inquired.

"Well, I think I just proved I can," I answered.

The officer laughed. Then my mother explained that she was riding along to make sure I could drive, but that she wasn't paying attention to the speed.

"It's a brand new car," she said. "It just didn't seem like he was going that fast."

"Well, okay," the officer said.

He let us go. He didn't write a ticket or even a warning. I think he was too surprised when he saw me behind the wheel.

It wasn't long before I was driving myself to school every day. Driving was no problem, but I needed some assistance to get out of the car. When I arrived at the school, the secretary would come out to my car and open the door. Otherwise I was trapped. It was a bit humiliating, but what other choice was there?

One day I really did get stuck. I got home from school and no one was around to let me out of the car. I sat there for awhile, then decided to try opening the door with my foot. I kicked off my shoe and made a few attempts. Fortunately, I'm very limber in my legs. I was able to get in the right position and finally got the door open.

By the time prom arrived I was set. I had a date and a car I could drive. My biggest fear was that I would look like a fool when I tried to dance. But doesn't everyone suffer from the same feeling? In my case, however, the press was going to be there.

A reporter and photographer from *People Magazine* came for about a week around prom time. The photographer's name was Taro Yamasaki, and my family and I got to know Taro quite well. He was assigned to shoot the cover photo for the May 1992 issue of People. That spring, Johnny Carson announced he was retiring from the Tonight show.

As a result, Johnny was on the cover of that May issue and I was featured in a less prominent story on the inside instead. I jokingly told Taro I was sore about Carson stealing my cover shot.

Our senior prom was on April 25th. Taro covered the event and joined in the festivities. My date, was my girlfriend Shaila, who was a member of the junior class. She was a good sport for putting up with the media attention. But Taro acted like he was one of us, so everyone felt at ease.

Taro made a number of other trips to our farm. I managed to get revenge for being bumped from the cover of *People*. When Taro and the *People Magazine* staff were visiting, we'd come up with farm chores they could do. It was a novelty for the press to travel to such a remote area of the world. To them, the wide open spaces, scarcity of traffic, and quiet were as foreign as the Australian outback. They considered doing farm chores to be another aspect of the adventure. We even had them working in the garden and digging potatoes. I don't think they ever complained.

Up to this point I'd attended a few public gatherings in or around Hurdsfield. I hadn't been too worried about being out in public because people were protective of me around home. So far, most of the experiences had been positive. Other than the spring music contest, I hadn't attended any big events away from home.

Before graduation I received a telephone call inviting me to attend a boxing match in Bismarck. The invitation was extended by Virgil Hill, a local middleweight fighter who was a title contender at the time. I thought it sounded like fun, especially since I would be a guest of Virgil's, and I could take some of my friends. I decided to take three of my classmates – Darnell, Jesse and Tim.

The closer we got to the day of the fight, the more nervous I got. For starters, my friends wanted to get to Bismarck early enough before the fight so they could eat something. I wanted to go later because I still couldn't feed myself and I was worried about what I'd do if I needed to use a rest room. I didn't want to be caught in an awkward situation, so I kept making excuses about why we should leave later. One of the guys took a quarter out of his pocket.

"Let's flip a coin, and the winner gets to feed John when we get to Bismarck."

I thought it was funny, and it showed me that my friends were sensitive enough to know I was worried about eating in public. I conceded the the argument, and we left early.

On the way to Bismarck, I told my friend Jesse that I might have him take the driver's seat once we got to the city. It's not like traffic in Bismarck is ever heavy — but I thought there might be more cars than usual since the fight was in town. It seemed like a good idea to let Jesse drive since I was still getting acclimated to driving after my accident.

When we got to Bismarck, everyone was hungry. They wanted to go to Pizza Hut for pizza. Even though I was hungry, I didn't want my friends to feed me in public.

"I'm not really hungry. I'll just drop you at Pizza Hut," I said. "While you're eating, I'll go visit my Aunt Jo."

My friends said, "No way."

"Stay with us. Even if you're not hungry you can sit and visit with us."

They ordered a pizza.

The waitress brought our pizza to the table and the guys each grabbed a slice. I was sitting there talking to Jesse and not paying a lot of attention to the food. Without my asking, Darnell held a piece of pizza in front of my mouth.

"What are you doing," I said trying to sound nonchalant.

"I know you're hungry, so I'll feed you," he said like it was no big deal and he did this all the time.

I just looked back at him and started laughing. I had to quit laughing before I started eating, otherwise I might have choked. After I took the first bite, I almost started crying because it was such a caring thing for him to do. It was the first time someone other than my family, health care workers, or hospital employees had fed me. Darnell acted like feeding me was no big deal, but it was to me.

After we finished our pizza, we drove to the Bismarck Civic Center to see the fight. Since we were special guests, we were ushered to our seats near the ring. The management had agreed to provide some security precautions in case I got mobbed. By now, I was learning to plan on the unpredictable. Even so, the best plans can go awry.

There was a match before the main event of the evening. In between the fights, the announcer asked me to step into the ring so I could be introduced to the crowd. I hadn't calculated how difficult it would be getting between the ropes and I almost tripped as I got in. I waved to the crowd and gave the photographers a chance to snap a few shots before I returned to my seat. Then the ring girls came over to where my friends and I were sitting so they could have their picture taken with us. We all thought that was just as good as getting to see the match.

Immediately following the fight, I was supposed to participate in a press conference with the fighter. During the final rounds of the fight, I was sizing up my escape route and looking for the security guards that were supposed to escort me to the press conference. We thought it was coordinated, but it was total chaos as soon as the fight was over. There were people coming at me from all directions. My friends did a great job of running interference and moving me through the crowd.

The security guards finally materialized — they were standing in another part of the arena and had trouble reaching us. I did the press conference and then my friends and I got ready to leave. We thought we were clear. Most of the spectators were gone and my friends and I were standing around talking on the arena floor. That's when a woman came out of nowhere. She grabbed me around the chest and started sobbing and crying uncontrollably. She had her arms wrapped so tightly around me that I would have had a hard time freeing myself from her grip even before my accident. It scared the hell out of me.

The woman simply wouldn't let go. I didn't want to offend her, but it was a very uncomfortable experience and I was totally helpless. Darnell was grabbing her arms trying to free me from her bear hug. My friends finally got her off me, explaining it could potentially hurt me to be hugged like that. They got her going on her way and then we made a fast exit.

I was really happy to be back home after the experience. Even though I had fun, the evening had been exhausting. In addition, I hadn't used the bathroom since we'd left Hurdsfield and I felt like I was going to explode. I was becoming aware that I couldn't always anticipate the reaction strangers might have when seeing me in public. Most people are naturally respectful of personal space. But there would always be the chance someone would act like the woman who grabbed me and wouldn't let go.

After the night of the fight, I started feeling better about socializing at school. I wasn't nearly as self conscious about having lunch with my friends on school days. We'd head to Lee's Café during the noon hour and it didn't bother me at all to be fed in public. It even got to the point where my friends would argue about who got to feed me, because they all wanted the honor.

Darnell, Jesse and I made another trip to Bismarck later that spring to shop for graduation gifts for our classmates. We were eating at McDonald's and Jesse was feeding me. There was a man sitting at the table next to us who kept staring at me. I'd meet his gaze and he would quickly turn away, but as soon as I looked away he'd start staring at me again.

Darnell noticed and he didn't think the man was being polite. Darnell started staring back. The guy looked away for a bit but started staring at me again.

"What's your problem?" Darnell asked him.

The man never answered, but Darnell kept staring back and eventually the guy got up and left.

Things got even more interesting when we went to the mall to do our shopping. People kept approaching me to chat and wish me well. It reached the point where we didn't think we'd get any shopping done. Darnell and Jesse decided to flank me as we walked through the mall. When necessary one of them would walk in front of me to break a path and disguise me. We finally got our shopping done and hurried to the car. I was relieved because I was worried that Darnell might beat someone up before we got out of the mall.

John Thompson, age 18. Senior photo taken in the fall of 1991.
(Swedlund Photography - Velva, ND)

Emergency room personnel at Harvey's St. Aloisius Hospital who aided John Thompson included (front left, back row) Dr. Curt Nyhus; Sister Celine; Twyla Laber, nurses aide; Corey Jones, physician assistant; and RNs Karen Volk and Joanie Martin. Front row: RNs Julie Keller, Cindy Rebenitsch and Lynda Roller. Treating John, they say, was an experience they will never forget.
(ND REC/RTC Magazine)

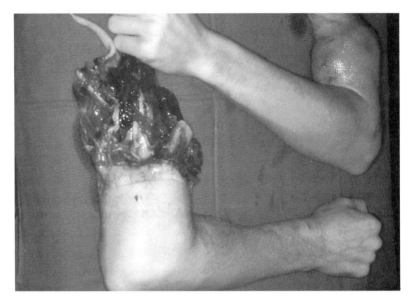

John's severed arms, cleaned and prepped for reattachment.
(North Memorial Medical Center photo)

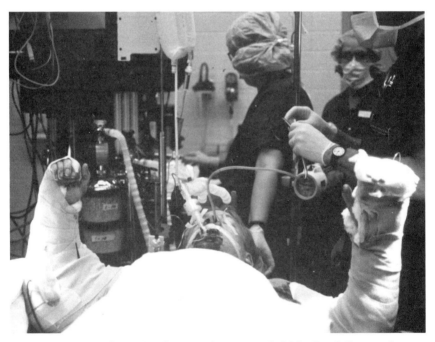

John, on a ventilator in the North Memorial Medical Center intensive care unit, following the initial reattachment surgery.
(North Memorial Medical Center photo courtesy ND REC/RTC Magazine)

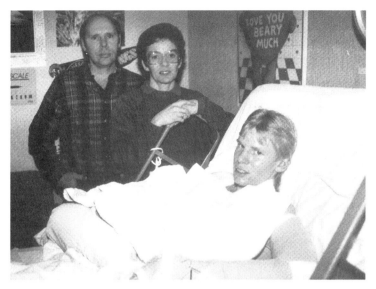

John with parents, Larry and Karen, on 7-West at North Memorial Medical Center.

(ND REC/RTC Magazine)

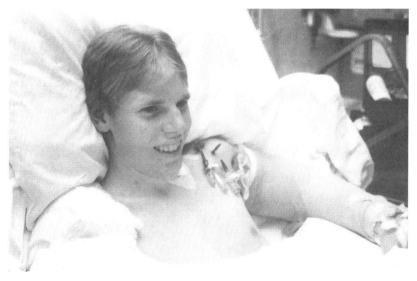

John's right arm was torn off at the shoulder, but his left arm suffered more damage. During reconstructive surgery to reattach his arms, skin grafts were used to cover blood vessels that ordinarily are covered by muscle tissue. Much of John's left arm muscle tissue was destroyed in the accident.

(ND REC/RTC Magazine)

A foot-operated control panel at North Memorial Medical Center designed especially for John.
(North Memorial Medical Center photo courtesy ND REC/RTC Magazine)

Emilio Estevez visited John several times while shooting a movie in Minneapolis. "He was great, real down to earth and caring," says John.

(Thompson family photo)

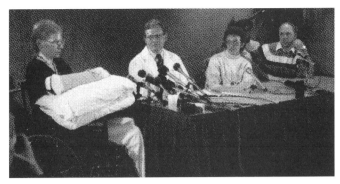

The first news conference in which John appeared before the national media on February 6, 1992. Earlier that day John did an exclusive interview with Joan Lunden.

(North Memorial Medical Center photo courtesy ND REC/RTC Magazine)

A sample of the mail and gifts that awaited John upon his homecoming.

(ND REC/RTC Magazine)

The North Memorial mailroom was flooded with thousands of cards and letters for John, many from foreign countries.
(North Memorial Medical Center photo courtesy ND REC/RTC Magazine)

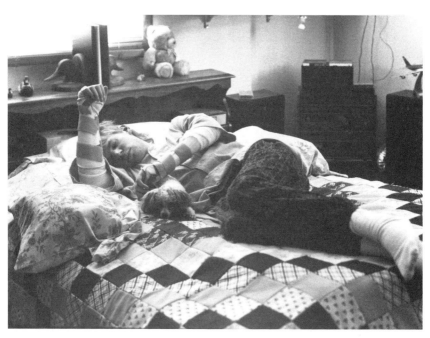

John with Tinker, the family poodle, in his bedroom at the farm.
(Photo by Taro Yamasaki)

John and best friend Tuffy stroll across a field on the family farm.
(Photo by Taro Yamasaki)

High school classmate and college roommate Darnell feeding John in April of 1992.

(Photo by Taro Yamasaki)

Dr. Allen Van Beek, parents Larry and Karen Thompson, and John being greeted by Minnesota Twins standout Kirby Puckett in the Hubert H. Humphrey Metrodome. Moments later John is seen on the big screen as he sings the National Anthem before the start of the ballgame. Summer 1992.

(Photo provided by North Memorial Medical Center)

John and Dr. Van Beek testified at the Great Plains Rural Health Summit sponsored by first lady Hillary Clinton in 1994. John highlighted the need for funding rural emergency services.

(White House Press Photo)

John and Tuffy with parents at home.

(Photo by Taro Yamasaki)

Letters of Hope

POSTMEN

If at all possible could you deliver this to the
young man living on a farm in North Dakota
U.S.A. who had both his arms ripped off in
an accident on the farm.

Thank you for all your help.

TO: Mr. ....
        .... Farm
        .Hurdfield N.D. 58451
        NORTH DAKOTA
        U.S.A.

Wayne Strom
Bangkok, Thailand

John Thompson
Hurdsfield, ND
USA

BY AIR MAIL
PAR AVION

By air mail
Par avion

the boy
N. Dakota

John Thompson (both arms lost in accident)
% North memorial Medical Centre.
Minneapolis. MINNESOTA
AMERICA.

Sent From:
48 Bunkers Hill Lane
Bilston West Midlands
England WV14 GJR

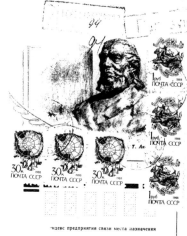

John Tompson
Herdsfield
North Dakota
USA (США)

454080
город- Челябинск-80
улица- Красная
дом- 42 кв. 23.
Евдокимову
Григорий Осипович

Индекс предприятия связи места назначения

Letter From: *Woman in Soviet Union*

Здравствуй дорогой Джон - Тöпсон !!
16 I-92 года мы прочитали в газете "Советская Россия" что с тобой произошло "большое горе, несчастье, с руками. Ты настоящий мужественный человек. Потерять вдруг обе руки. Это нас глубоко тронуло: парень молодой - школьник- старшего класса. Джон - дай Бог тебе терпения хорошего здоровья, успеха в лечении. Самое главное, чтобы было все хорошо после операции. Дай Бог тебе полного выздоровления. Тебе пишут пенсионеры из города Челябинска. Нам по 81 году мы верующие. Усердно молимся за тебя. Господу Богу, Иисусу Христу, чтобы Господь Бог помог тебе поправиться, исцелиться от этого горя, и недуга. Мы молимся за тебя каждый день. И читаем Акафист святителю Николаю. Он помогает в беде и горе.
У нас два сына, - Один врач, другой военный - на пенсии, подполковник.
Джон - пусть напишут нам твои родители о твоём здоровьи... мы будем очень рады.
Наш Адрес город Челябинск 80
Индекс.   улица Красная
454080   дом 42 кв 23.
Евдокимову Григорий
Осипович.
с Уважением - Любовь Георгиевна

21 января 1992 г.

Chapter 8
Graduation

Graduation day was Sunday, May 17th. We had several parties planned in the final ten days leading up to the conclusion of our high school careers.

The first event was on a Friday night the week before graduation. My friend Lee Anne was the host. She lived on a farm and her parents were home to keep an eye on the festivities. They made us turn in our car keys as soon as we arrived and they checked us to make sure it was safe for us to drive. They wanted to make sure anyone who was drinking and got drunk, couldn't get behind the wheel. Those were the rules. We had a great time. About 70 people showed up, including a number of parents who were invited.

Our second party was a week later. A band from Bismarck had contacted me earlier and asked if they could play for me sometime. I asked them if they would be interested in doing the music for our senior party. They agreed, even though the party was scheduled for the same day two of the band members were celebrating their wedding anniversary.

I asked the owners of the Corner Bar in Hurdsfield if we could hold the party there. My folks supplied one of our pigs for the event. We butchered it and roasted it whole on a big rotisserie. Other families supplied salads and desserts. It was an impressive smorgasbord. We even ordered an anniversary cake to show our appreciation to the band for agreeing to play.

The party was a big community event. Several of my friends from

Minnesota made the trip to Hurdsfield, too. They stayed to attend the graduation ceremony. To ensure there were no problems, an off-duty police officer was hired for security. The press was also there.

By the time I arrived at the party there was a camera man from NBC News, New York waiting for me. I'll admit I tipped a few before I got to the bar, as had most of my class. I asked the guy not to get any of us drinking on tape, and he agreed he wouldn't, but after a couple more drinks I didn't really care what he filmed. Neither did he. He was waving his $30,000 camera around, filming upside down and sideways. Like my friends Jay and Ron from Minneapolis, he couldn't believe the drinks cost only about a third as much as the price in big city bars. They just figured they could drink three times as much.

After the party was over, everyone spent Saturday getting ready for graduation, and in some cases, nursing hangovers. The school administration insisted on holding the graduation ceremony in the gymnasium even though our class would have preferred to have the ceremony outside. We were concerned it would get overcrowded and hot inside. I think the administration underestimated how much local and media interest there would be in the ceremony. When Sunday arrived, the street outside the school was filled with satellite trucks and vans. It was a circus.

At home, the phone was ringing off the wall. Reporters were calling to request exclusive interviews. News people kept "dropping in" at the farm. My brother managed, rather innocently, to frighten a few of them off. He was outside doing some target shooting with his pistol. Some news people drove in the yard, saw him with his gun, and turned right around without stopping.

A number of press people called to ask if they could come to the house to take pictures of me getting ready for the graduation ceremonies. Thankfully, Jay was there. He took control of the situation as far as the media were concerned. He fielded calls and organized a press conference to be held after the ceremony at my reception. Even so, it was chaotic. The constant ringing of the phone was giving all of us headaches, and I swear I'd finish one call and the phone would start ringing before I got the receiver hung up.

I drove myself into town for the ceremony. My family and Jay had gotten a head start and were already at the school. Once I arrived, I couldn't see how I was going to get in the building. I cruised by and then drove to my grandmother's house so I could call Jay at the school. We had to figure out some sort of plan for sneaking me inside.

We decided to have Ron drive over to my grandmother's. He touched up my hair, then drove me back to the school where Jay had organized a group of people to escort me into the building. Ron stopped the car, and I stepped out. The press caught sight of me and started stampeding in my direction. My escorts hustled me inside and guided me to the room where the rest of the graduates were getting ready. The reporters followed close behind.

There were windows in the doors of the room. To give the graduates privacy, someone covered the glass with paper — but they had taped the paper on the outside. The reporters and photographers just ripped it off and started taking pictures. We got people to stand in front of the windows, but then the press ran outside the building so they could take pictures through the outside windows. When we pulled the curtains there wasn't much more they could do, so they just stayed by the classroom door waiting for someone to come or go so they could try to sneak in. They'd claim to be family members or friends of one of the graduates, but they kept forgetting that in small towns everybody knows everyone else.

We finally lined up for our procession into the gym. I was the next to last person in line. When I started walking into the gym it was like walking into a room lit by strobe lights. There were hundreds of camera flashes. The press had been corralled in the back of the gym in a section that was roped off from family and friends.

There were the usual words of greeting by the school principal and then I was supposed to sing a song. Before the music started I said, "I dedicate this song to my teachers, friends, family, and especially my classmates."

I started to choke up but I managed to get the rest of the dedication out. "I probably wouldn't be graduating today if it wasn't for you. Thanks for all your help and support."

I sang "One Moment in Time" by Whitney Houston. I could see a couple of my classmates were crying. After I finished, I told my class I loved them and sat back down. Everyone started applauding. Then Darnell stood, and the whole auditorium went to their feet for a standing ovation. All my classmates except Darnell came up to me and we shared a group hug. Darnell was too overcome with emotion to join in the hug. He was afraid he'd break down and start crying. It was one of the greatest moments of my life, and I was grateful to be there to share it with my friends.

We got our diplomas and after the recessional everyone went outside for the traditional receiving line. In small towns everyone likes to extend congratulations. I was standing between Darnell and Lee Anne. They worked out a plan for keeping the line moving. If someone stopped in front of me for too long, Darnell would get them moving on their way with a firm nudge.

The receiving line was the most stressful part of the day. While my classmates were careful about touching me, for some reason other people felt they had to pat me on the shoulders or arms. At this point in my recovery, I was hypersensitive in my arms. Anything more than a gentle touch could be quite painful. But a number of people seemed oblivious to that.

After the ceremony there was a big reception for the Hurdsfield students in my class at the Hurdsfield community center. The Bowdon students had their reception in Bowdon. Jay had all the press come to the community center for a formal press conference. Everyone was interested in how it felt to graduate with my class.

Ron and Jay had flown Ron's small plane to Hurdsfield from Minneapolis. That afternoon, Ron flew Darnell, Jesse, Michelle, Kristen and I from the Harvey airport to Bismarck. We rented a limousine and toured the town.

While graduation was a reason to celebrate, it was also a time for good-byes. A couple days later my friend Darnell left for National Guard basic training. Kristen and I drove him to Jamestown to catch his bus. He was going to be gone for the entire summer, and many of my other class-mates would be going away. It was another adjustment, and another layer of security was gone. But it was also a sign that life was moving forward. Before Darnell left he introduced me to cute little blonde he knew from Harvey. Her name was Lisa and we hit it off immediately. We spent the next few weeks getting to know each other better and that helped me deal with my classmates' departure.

Chapter 9
Rehabilitation

Just as my classmates went their separate ways, I also had to leave home to work on my rehabilitation program over the summer. On June 20th, I left for Courage Center, a facility in Golden Valley, Minnesota. My parents drove me to the center, and helped me unpack my belongings. We filled out all of the admission paperwork, then I told them to leave. I wanted them to go before I changed my mind. I wasn't sure I wanted to stay. I knew that if my parents lingered long enough, I'd end up talking them into taking me back home.

My parents' feelings were hurt when I told them to leave. I'm not very good at saying goodbye and I think they were convinced I was upset with them. In truth, I was simply scared. Most of the people at Courage Center were in wheelchairs. Many had spinal injuries, or closed brain injuries with permanent brain damage. Some of the residents had lost their capacity to speak. A few of them were able to use computerized devices to help them communicate, but some were only capable of making strange noises and it was impossible to understand what they were trying to say.

From the beginning, I knew my stay at Courage Center would be an adjustment. It also made me appreciate the fact that I hadn't suffered a head or spinal cord injury. The challenges I faced were much easier in comparison.

The nurses and staff at Courage Center were very caring. I especially liked the secretary. She was in her thirties and her name was Eileen. She was married and had kids. I considered her my substitute mom while I was at Courage Center. At any rate, she was someone I could talk to.

When I first arrived at Courage Center, I was hesitant to spend time in the community areas. I preferred the quiet and privacy of my own room. The staff, however, felt socializing with the other residents was an important part of my care plan. They kept trying to persuade me to join the other residents for meals, activities or television. Eventually, I became more comfortable outside my room, but I usually spent my free time visiting with Eileen. That is, until she started falling behind on her responsibilities and would tell me she had to get some work done.

In an effort to prod me out of my solitude, the nurses tried to get me to play "Pictionary" with the group. The game involves drawing pictures so I wasn't very excited about the idea. Since I couldn't use my hands to draw, I told them "no thanks."

They wouldn't take no for an answer.

"We're all going to put the pencils in our mouths and draw the pictures that way," said one of the nurses.

Everyone else agreed to the idea but I told them, "Thanks for the effort, but I'm not really into games."

Looking back, I was a difficult resident. The staff, to their credit, were very patient and understanding.

My second week at Courage Center, I began occupational and physical therapy sessions. Physical therapy involved a lot of flexing and extending of the muscles in my arms. It wasn't hard work, but sometimes it was extremely frustrating. When I couldn't get a muscle to do what it was supposed to do, we had to figure out why it wasn't working. It was like some weird puzzle. It was even worse when I could perform a movement one time, but couldn't repeat it.

Basically, the difficulties arose from internal wiring problems. When the doctors reattached my muscles and nerves, things weren't hooked up like they had been before the accident. The result was that when I would attempt to move my pinky, my thumb moved instead. Then, when I wanted to move my thumb, I'd have to adjust my thought process. My brain would have to remember it was actually the same as moving my pinky and send that message in order to make my thumb move.

I had problems with sensation, too. For example, my finger would itch — at least that's how my brain interpreted the feeling. Instead of scratching my finger, I'd have to scratch my elbow. Again, the connections were different so my brain was fooled into thinking it was my finger that itched when in reality it was my elbow. My therapist and I spent a lot of time trying to retrain my brain to interpret messages and figure out where everything was.

It's hard to describe how odd all this conscious compensation seemed. The brain, however, is an amazing tool. Even though the circuits were all mixed up, eventually I learned how to appropriately decode the inputs and respond with the correct output.

Occupational therapy was designed to help me find ways to perform activities of daily living such as dressing, eating and bathing. At home, I got help with these things, but I didn't want to be dependent for the rest of my life. I felt I had a lot at stake, so it was disappointing when things didn't progress as fast as I hoped.

The first task I worked on in occupational therapy was dressing myself. I didn't know it could be such hard work. I could pull my jeans on, but buttoning them or zipping them was impossible. We tried putting some Velcro on them to hold them shut, but it wasn't exactly the fashion statement I wanted to make. Eventually we found a small hook called a "Zip" that worked to pull up the zipper tab. With a lot of practice, I was able to get my jeans on completely by myself.

Getting a shirt on proved to be more of a challenge. At this point in my recovery, I was still wearing splints on my arms, and my range of motion was very limited. At first, we found the easiest way to get shirts that buttoned on, was to leave them buttoned up and pull them over my head like a t-shirt. Getting a shirt on was much easier than taking it off. Since I didn't have the use of my hands, I had to wriggle my head down inside of the shirt and then grab it in between my knees and pull it off. Occasionally the shirt would get stuck. It felt like I was trapped inside a cloth bag.

Bathing was the least of our troubles. The staff sewed a wash cloth into a mitten, which I attached to my hand with a Velcro strap. It had a mesh pocket that held a bar of soap so I could strapped the mitt on, and scrub myself into a good lather. They also found pump bottles to dispense shampoo and conditioner.

While bathing was easy, feeding myself was the most difficult activity. I was motivated to keep working at it because I didn't want to be fed by someone else for the rest of my life. I was especially intimidated by the prospect of eating in public. People would inevitably stare at me. I found if I explained my situation, most restaurants would try to accommodate me at a private table. Some of them went out of their way. For instance, one restaurant had spoons with handles that were too wide to fit my adaptive straps. They called around to several competitors to locate utensils that would work.

During my time at Courage Center, the therapists and I tried a number of approaches to make it easier for me to feed myself. First, we tried working on the traditional approach of holding a fork in my hand. I simply couldn't grasp it. Then we tried attaching the fork to my hand with an inch wide Velcro strap. It worked fine for keeping the fork on my hand and for stabbing the food, but I wasn't able to rotate my wrist to the proper angle to get the food into my mouth. We tried bending the forks to different angles. All we ended up with was a pile of twisted metal. Then we tried forks that could swivel on the strap. If I tried to stab the food, the fork swiveled away and I couldn't pick anything up. If by chance I succeeded in stabbing the food, by the time I raised the fork to my mouth, it would swivel away and I couldn't get it in.

Back home, my parents were getting flack from some people who accused them of "dumping" me in Minneapolis. Everyone's entitled to their opinion, but too many people felt they should impose their views on my family. There were those who thought mom and dad should have stayed in the cities with me while I was at Courage Center. Of course, they didn't know (or care) that it was my choice to stay there on my own. Besides, my parents had a farm to run.

My goal was total independence, something a lot of people couldn't comprehend. How could a farm kid, who'd had his arms ripped off in an accident, ever be totally independent? To me, it wasn't a question of whether or not it was possible — it was a question of how soon it would be possible.

After mastering the basics of feeding myself, I also needed to learn how to cook for myself. I didn't want to starve, and I wasn't comfortable with the thought of eating in restaurants for the rest of my life. Eileen was invaluable in helping me master the kitchen. Since I couldn't use my thumbs, I learned to crack an egg by dropping it on the counter in just the right way. My first baking effort was a pan of chocolate brownies, which I was proud to let everyone sample. Eileen, of course, got the first one.

The splints stayed on my arms until July. They held my arms in a bent or flexed position, but the time had come to work on straightening or extending them. After six months of wearing them, I was excited about getting the splints off. They were cumbersome and heavy. I was also a little reluctant. The splints afforded protection in case my arms got bumped.

When the splints were removed, my arms felt strange. I had grown accustomed to the extra weight and now my arms almost felt detached because they were so light. It was disconcerting. My arms were also frozen in an "L" shape. Physical therapy concentrated on the process of stretching. The therapist would put one of his or her hands under my elbow. Using the other hand, they would exert downward pressure on my hand and forearm. It was somewhat painful, but tolerable. What really got to me were the sounds my joints made as we went through the exercises. The popping, grating and groaning were just plain creepy.

Because my arms were so rigid, the therapists were concerned they might break bones if they pushed too hard. There were times when they were pushing really hard, and I couldn't resist the opportunity to play a practical joke. The therapist would be concentrating on my forearm, and I'd let my elbow slip back. It would appear that my arm had just gone straight, and I'd start screaming, "You broke it! You broke my arm!" The therapists fell for it every time. Their faces would freeze with fear. When they realized I was joking around, they usually didn't think it was all that funny, even though I got a laugh out of it.

We didn't make the progress we'd hoped with the stretching, so I was fitted for a new type of splint that applied opposing pressure on my arm. The thing was spring loaded to keep my elbow straightened, but it was horribly uncomfortable. I hated wearing it, but Eileen encouraged me to give it some time. After a few weeks, I still wasn't seeing any benefit and decided the splint wasn't worth it. I was willing to work hard at stretching the muscles myself, and I thought I'd probably have better results.

I would place my elbow against the inside of my knee and position my hand on the inside of my ankle. Then I'd press with all my strength and the joints would give a little snap. With each crack or pop my arm would go a little straighter. It was kind of scary at first because I was afraid I might do some actual damage, but in the end it worked a lot better than the splints. I also knew how much pain and discomfort I could tolerate better than my therapists did, so I could exert more pressure and get quicker results. I never did tell my doctor about my method, so he thought the straightening was the result of wearing the splints.

It took a considerable amount of time to get my elbows unfrozen and straightened. They will never be perfectly straight, and I will never have complete mobility, but I'm confident my method achieved a better outcome than if I had continued to wear the splints.

Next, I had to start working on my wrists. They were also frozen in position, but they were straight. I would put my fist on my leg with my lower arm straight to the elbow. Then I would push downward and out with as much strength as I could. I was startled when my wrist released with a loud pop. The joint was free but sore, and I was concerned that I might have broken something. But I soon discovered I could move my wrist outward. I tried pushing down again — this time with inward pressure. Another pop and my wrist was free so I could move it up and down. I did the same thing for the other arm.

As it turned out, the reason my joints were frozen was an unintended result of wearing the splints. My arms had been in the same position for so long that calcium deposits had formed in the joints. I should also caution anyone reading this, that taking matters into my own hands was not the wisest course of action. I could have done serious damage to my joints. Fortunately, my frustration and impatience didn't have any bad consequences.

During my stay at Courage Center, things weren't all work. I had a fair amount of leisure time and many of the friends I'd made at North Memorial Hospital came to visit. I was also free to go out on pass and tour the Minneapolis/St. Paul area. Thanks to Jay, Lori and Ron, I made frequent trips away from Courage Center and I got to know the city well. I really liked what it had to offer, and considered moving there. Coming from a farm, exploring the metro area was an adventure. We went to the science museum, movies, and nightclubs. Almost every place we went, people recognized me. The businesses were very gracious and our meals, drinks, or tickets were usually complimentary.

Later in the summer, my parents brought my car down to the cities, so I could get around on my own. It did a lot to bolster my sense of independence. Once my elbows and wrists were loose and mobile, it was much easier to feed myself, and get dressed. I could make use of the adaptive forks, I figured out how to cook, and I was starting to plan for my return home. I also started to think about college, something Dr. Van Beek insisted I should do.

During my stay at Courage Center, I got a call from the Minnesota Twins Baseball organization. They were aware that I liked to sing, and asked if I would sing the National Anthem at a home game in the Hubert H. Humphrey Metrodome. I was really excited because it was something I had always wanted to do. While I was still at North Memorial in Robbinsdale my mother and I had watched the Super Bowl Game and I had commented that I hadn't cared for the way the National Anthem had been performed. My mother prophetically told me, "Someday you might be the one singing the anthem for a pro game." I never thought it would happen, but now I had my chance.

I called everyone I knew to let them know I would be singing at the Twins game on July 27th. I wanted to get the music just right, so I rehearsed with the music therapist at Courage Center. I tried several different styles. I dressed it up a little, then a little more. Then I decided to bring it back down a notch. We worked on it until we thought it sounded polished and professional.

The Twins management must have released the story to the press notifying them I would be singing the anthem. Soon, the media were flooding Courage Center with calls requesting interviews, or asking to tape and photograph my rehearsals. I obliged a few of them.

The day of the game, most of my family and a lot of my friends came to Minneapolis. A lot of the staff from North Memorial, including Dr. Van Beek and Jay, came to the stadium to hear me sing. The Metrodome provided us with good security. There had been a lot of advance publicity, and everyone knew I would be singing the anthem. I was escorted to the locker room where the Twins players were getting dressed for the game and I was introduced to several of the players before I got a brief explanation of what was going to happen.

There was still time to meet with the press and visit with my family and friends before I went out on the field. I had no idea how many people the Metrodome could seat, until it was announced there were 67,000 people in the stands for the game. By now, my mother was a nervous wreck. In fact, she was more anxious than she was for some of my surgeries. For some strange reason, I felt incredibly calm. Singing in front of such a large live audience and on national television didn't scare me. My mother was scared enough for both of us.

A friend of my mother's, (who was also the wife of Rick, my ambulance driver), asked my mother to get Kent Hrbek's autograph for her if she had the opportunity. Patsy was a huge Hrbek fan, and this was supposed to be her birthday present.

In spite of her case of nerves, my mother got up the courage to ask for the autograph. The only problem was, she didn't know which player was Kent Hrbek. Someone pointed Kent out to my mother, so she hurried over to him to see if she could get him to sign. In her excitement she blurted out, "Aren't you Kirby Puckett?"

For those of you who don't follow baseball or the Minnesota Twins, there is a vast difference between Kirby Puckett and Kent Hrbek. Kirby is black and Kent is white.

My mother realized her error immediately and was ready to crawl under the nearest available seat. She was making sincere apologies, but Hrbek wasn't pleased. He spat out a huge wad of chewing tobacco, which landed close to mom's foot, and then he stalked off. Patsy did not get her autograph, but after hearing the story I doubt she was quite so enamored of Hrbek.

Just before the game started, my parents, Dr. Van Beek, Jay and I were escorted down the long corridor leading out to the field. Since "Beek" had gone first at all of our joint press conferences, I joked with him, "This time you follow me."

Once on the field, the announcer introduced all of us. Standing at home plate, I finally realized how big the stadium was and how many people were in the stands. I'm sure we looked like tourists in the big city for the first time. Then we noticed ourselves on the huge closed circuit television screen. My parents were waving in the general direction of where our friends and family were seated, but we couldn't distinguish them in the crowd. Then, the real Kirby Puckett came onto the field and presented me with a Minnesota Twins jersey emblazoned with my name and number while photographers snapped our picture.

It was amazing that while I stood there, surrounded by tens of thousands of baseball fans, I wasn't nervous. I was more concerned that if I stood too close to my mom, her nervousness would rub off on me.

I had been alerted to expect an echo inside the dome, but I had not had the opportunity to rehearse with their sound system or acoustics. I started the first few bars and it was going great until my own voice bounced back at me. It disoriented me for only a second, but I didn't get lost. I finished the anthem. There was a brief pause, and then a loud roar of noise came up from the crowd and everyone rose to their feet for a standing ovation. I looked over at my parents and they were both crying, but I just stood there with a smile. Then we walked off the field.

My immediate family and I were treated to a private box with an assortment of food and beverages. There were also two televisions. The rest of my family and friends were seated as a group in the general seats, but they took turns coming up to visit us in the box.

My mother finally started to relax and enjoy herself. We all had a great time — except the Twins. The team lost the game in what became a losing streak. There was even a rumor that I had jinxed them, but it wasn't anything I took seriously. After the game, we returned to our hotel and everyone went down to the bar to relax. The local television news came on, with clips of me singing the national anthem. We celebrated the occasion, and the hotel let us have full access to the bar, including self-service for the drinks.

The morning following the game, my mother's good mood dissolved. We picked up the morning Minneapolis Tribune, which shouted the bold headline, "JOHN THOMPSON SINGS NATIONAL ANTHEM AND NERVOUS MOTHER MISTAKES KENT HRBEK FOR KIRBY PUCKET." She had lots of unkind words for the press, but the rest of us thought it was humorous. We still tease mom about her mistake, and now even she can laugh about it.

There were other highlights during my summer at Courage Center. Every year, the Twin Cities host a celebrity softball tournament for charity. A variety of professional sports teams are recruited to participate. I was asked if I would serve as the honorary softball coach for the Pittsburgh Steelers. My friend Jesse was flown to Minneapolis, and he got to be the honorary assistant coach.

I also did my first professional video that summer. Dr. Van Beek started a program called "First Care" to address safety and trauma issues. I worked on a farm safety video for the program.

Thanks to my friends from North Memorial Hospital, it was a good summer and my stay at Courage Center passed quickly. Lori, Jay and Ron made sure I wasn't bored. Lori even took me to Valley Fair, a large amusement park outside of Minneapolis. I wasn't wearing my splints, so I didn't have a great deal of control over my arms. We decided to go on the "Octopus" which spins while rotating up and down. My arms were flying up and down, almost like they weren't a part of my body. Suddenly, my right arm snapped back and smacked me square in the face. If it hadn't been so freakish, it would have been hysterical. Lori was trying to make sure I was okay at the same time she was trying not to laugh.

After the Octopus, we decided to try the swinging chairs. The ride looked tame enough — until we got in. Each person sits in their own seat, which is suspended from a center hub by chains. The chairs rotate around the center hub. Everything was fine until we picked up momentum. The seats started to tilt forward and backward. I couldn't hang on and nearly fell out when the seats were tilted forward. I was screaming for help, and Lori was screaming for the operator to stop the ride. Of course, he couldn't hear us.

When the ride finally did stop, Lori came running over to see if I was all right. She started laughing, but it took me a while to think it was funny. We've been to Valley Fair several times since then, and I always joke about riding the swinging chairs. The truth is, I'll stick with the Octopus.

My stay at Courage Center helped me build confidence and equipped me with many of the skills I needed to be independent. I knew that as much as my parents wanted to help me, I couldn't burden them with that kind of obligation. The strain of my accident and the trips they had to make to Minnesota for my follow-up care were putting them behind on the farm work. They never complained about it, but I knew it was stressful. In addition, my brother Mick moved off the farm in early August to start a new job. If I couldn't lend help with the farm work, the least I could do was make sure I wasn't an obstacle to getting it done.

My parents were still receiving mail from people who criticized them for not staying with me while I was at Courage Center. This would continue to be a theme among a certain group of people. There was always some busybody waiting to tell my family and I how to live our lives.

Chapter 10
College

After my accident, I received numerous college scholarship offers. Notre Dame, a college in Florida, The University of North Dakota, and North Dakota State University even extended full tuition scholarships. I basically had my choice of schools, and Dr. Van Beek was lobbying persistently for me to enroll in college in the fall.

Personally, I had reservations. Most of the scholarship offers were from large schools in other states. In light of my situation, I wanted to be within a reasonable distance of Minneapolis. I would require follow-up care with Dr. Van Beek and the team at North Memorial. I also was concerned about the type of support system I would have at school. Would there be people who knew me? Would I be able to be independent? When I needed special accommodations, would the school help me plan around those needs? Would the school and other students be able to deal constructively with my notoriety?

My biggest concern was that I simply wasn't ready for the demands of college. My last semester of high school was a blur. I had to expend a great deal of energy on my physical rehabilitation program. It would have been better if I'd had more time to prepare.

Several of my high school friends were planning to stay in the area. There was a junior college as well as a private university in Bismarck. The university had a strong music program and I was considering pursuing a major in music. Darnell was planning to enroll there, so we drove down to Bismarck to look at the campus. They sounded willing to work with me, so I decided to enroll, even though I didn't receive as significant a scholarship offer as some of the others.

The University of Mary is a Catholic college. It's run by the Benedictine sisters who came to Bismarck back in the days of Dakota Territory. In 1885, they started the first hospital in the Territory, St. Alexius.

The sisters eventually located their priory or monastery about six miles south of Bismarck on bluffs overlooking the Missouri River. In 1955, they started a two-year Catholic girls' college which is located at the same site. Over the years the educational programs were expanded to include four-year degrees and masters degree programs. Oh, they also decided to become a co-ed institution.

The college is small. That was an attraction, although it made it more likely I would be noticed, and I didn't want to be conspicuous. I thought the professors and staff would be apt to take a personal interest in the students.

The school assigned Darnell and me to a dorm room equipped with its own bathroom and shower. We started to get excited about the idea of going to college together. Even so, when the end of August arrived, I was nervous about starting.

Darnell and I got moved into our room with the help of our families. Then we went shopping and bought all the usual "guy" stuff — beer posters, centerfolds, a black light, a dorm refrigerator, and other necessities. We tried to make the room "homey" and even got a couch and some old carpeting to cover the tile floor.

There was an orientation session for all the freshmen students, which was supposed to be an opportunity to become acquainted with the campus as well as a chance to get to know people. It went a lot differently than I expected it would. The publicity surrounding my accident made me well-known even before my first class. I didn't know anyone there except Darnell — but everyone knew me. Students would approach me and start talking to me as though we were life-long friends. I had expected people to be stand-offish, but that wasn't the case at all.

It was nice that people weren't afraid to talk to me, but I was at a disadvantage because the students rarely told me their names. I wouldn't have remembered them all anyway. I only got to know a few close friends by name, and that was usually only by first names. People would pass me in the hall and say, "Hi, John. How are you?" I wouldn't have a clue about who they were.

The first year after my accident, my memory was sketchy. When someone greeted me, I often didn't know whether I had met that person before. I'd be asking myself, "Should I know his (her) name, or are they just being friendly?" It was disconcerting, and I was anxious about leaving my room or being in social situations.

It didn't take long for me to get in trouble at the University of Mary. There was a strictly enforced "no alcohol on campus policy." Within 48 hours of my arrival at the University, I got busted for having beer in my dorm room. Darnell and my cousin had purchased the beer. I didn't think it was good idea, but nevertheless it was in the room I shared with Darnell. That made me fifty percent responsible.

The resident assistant confiscated the brew and gave us a verbal warning. Of course, I was now at the top of his list of Freshman troublemakers. The incident also established my reputation as a heavy boozer although I didn't even have the opportunity to drink any of the stuff.

As far as being a heavy drinker, I won't deny I was under age, or that I drank. In comparison to a lot of students, however, I didn't drink much at all. In fact, the whole time I was at the University of Mary I attended only a handful of parties, all at my cousin Tina's. I certainly didn't earn the reputation I developed as a booze maniac. There were stories flying around that I hollowed out hiding places in the walls of my dorm room so I could stash my liquor. By the time I left the University of Mary, people had concocted stories that I was into drugs, too.

On weekends, I usually went home to the farm. I could spend time with Tuffy, my family, and Lisa. Harvest time is especially hectic, but the autumn after my accident I think my folks were overwhelmed. My brother got married in early October. I sang at the wedding. Even though it was a happy occasion, I think it was a very emotional time for my mother. In light of everything that had happened during the year, she was emotionally and physically exhausted.

As the harvest proceeded, it seemed like things just kept adding up. It would rain so my dad couldn't get the harvesting finished. Or the tractor would break down. The transmission went out in one of the trucks, and so on. I felt it was even more important that I become independent, and I didn't want my parents to worry about how I was doing.

Looking back at those first few months at the University of Mary, it was obvious I wasn't prepared for college. Mentally, I was suffering from the equivalent of a post-traumatic stress reaction. I reached the point where I didn't want to leave our dorm room, but Darnell worked very hard to keep me from becoming isolated. When he couldn't get me to leave the room, he'd bring friends in to meet me. Of course, they had to be screened and meet Darnell's rigorous standards before they could be introduced to me. Darnell just wanted to establish that these people weren't kooks, but I wonder if he didn't have some test he'd make them take before they could meet me.

Eventually, I did make a few friends. I met a girl, Jennifer, who convinced me that I'd have a lot more fun if I would go places and do things with her and her friends. Jennifer even got me to go to the cafeteria for dinner. Up until then, the cafeteria staff had been delivering my meals to me in my room. I was very self-conscious about eating in public with all my special straps and attachments. I didn't take every meal at the cafeteria, but Jennifer could talk me into going once in a while.

Darnell played basketball, so he got to know a lot of the guys in athletics at the University. He introduced me to some of the players who lived in our dorm, as well as our neighbors in the dorm room next door, Bob and Chad. Bob was a pre-nursing student and we got to be close friends. My experience as a patient gave us a lot to talk about. Darnell also introduced me to Mitch, a football player who lived down the hall in the dormitory.

When I made my decision to attend the University of Mary, my family and I had no idea it would be controversial. After I left for school, my parents started receiving letters criticizing them for not selling the farm and moving to Bismarck with me. Even though it had been seven months since my accident, my life and decisions were still very much in the public eye.

Perhaps I should have felt more pressure to perform academically. But, I never had been a stellar student. As I've said before, I simply wasn't ready for college. For that matter, college wasn't ready for me.

I dreaded going to classes. I was unable to take my own notes, so I had to rely on someone else. I couldn't write anything, so I had to take all of my tests orally. Some of my classmates thought the special treatment meant the teacher was coaching me or giving me some of the answers. If they had seen my grades, they would have been assured that I wasn't getting any help.

The point is, there was always some sort of rumor getting started. Being the subject of the rumors didn't help me emotionally or physically. Out of self-defense, I became a sort of recluse. I would go to classes, and then straight back to my room. People who are close to me now, find it difficult to believe that I was very quiet. But, no matter what I did, there was always some sort of negative story being concocted. No wonder I didn't want to leave my room.

For instance, I purchased a new pickup truck in the fall of 1992. Shortly after that, my family got letters criticizing me for not using the money to buy a new ambulance for the local rural ambulance service.

Some of the stories were plainly malicious. When I tried to socialize more, the rumor mill worked overtime. There were stories that I was some sort of sex maniac with multiple girlfriends and a taste for orgies. It was too ridiculous to be believed.

My friends picked up on a rumor that I was a doper and I was dealing drugs. We found out who started that one, but the story kept circulating. Considering all the medications I had to take after my accident, it was a miracle I didn't become addicted to something. I certainly never sold drugs. On the other hand, even the legally prescribed drugs have the potential to mess you up.

Another rumor was circulating that I walked around like I was better than everyone else. Someone told one of my friends they "hated" me because I was so cocky. It was aggravating because the person who said this had never met me. My friends were honest enough to tell me this guy had formed his opinion because of the way I walked. He thought I was strutting around.

After asking a few friends about my walk, they agreed — I did appear to be strutting. We put our heads together and analyzed the problem. After wearing the splints on my arms for so many months after my accident, I had grown accustomed to the extra weight. When the splints came off, my posture was way off. In addition, I had some residual stiffness in my left shoulder.

My friends agreed to coach me on my posture and gait, and I was able to walk better. But, the rumors persisted. There was even a rumor that I was drunk or stoned when I had my accident. I became increasingly frustrated and started spending even more time in my room. I didn't realize these rumors were mild compared with some of the stories that would circulate later.

Even though I went home almost every weekend, I didn't share any of my problems at school with my parents or with Lisa. I'd spend my weekends visiting friends, spending time with my dog and trying to relax. I didn't expect my parents to cope with my problems. I was trying to prove my independence. At the same time, I thought they had been through enough already. I didn't want to cause them any more grief. If they asked how things were going, I answered "okay" or "fine."

As the semester progressed, I rarely attended class. I quit eating, unless it was junk food. It seemed like I was living off Mountain Dew and Marlboro Light cigarettes. Since I was skinny to start with, this didn't do anything to build up my strength. In truth, I was falling into a deep depression. The farm boy whose story had given hope to others, was beginning to feel hopeless. It happened gradually, and insidiously so I wasn't aware of the change at first.

I became more distant from my family and from Lisa. Lisa was quite a bit younger than I was, and the fact that she was still in Harvey made it difficult to maintain a serious relationship. Eventually we broke up. While I felt the break-up was the right thing, it left me feeling more isolated and depressed.

You're probably wondering why no one alerted my parents to what was happening, or why the school wasn't aware of my depression. First, I hadn't given most of the faculty any clues. In fact, I had been assigned to an advisor when I started college. He was a priest, who helped me select my courses. He also taught an advisory group class that was mandatory for all freshmen. It was kind of an "I'm okay, you're okay" thing. I thought it was a waste of time and I refused to go. Of course, that made the priest angry. We weren't on solid footing, and he wasn't someone in whom I would confide.

I don't blame the college for not alerting my parents about what was going on. I didn't want my parents to know and I wasn't telling any campus staff how bad things were. As for my friends — they knew I'd be angry if they called my parents. They kept hoping things would get better, but they didn't know what else to do. It wasn't an easy situation for them.

After I started college, I missed class because of numerous medical appointments. I had more surgery and the recovery always took a lot out of me. I was also scheduled for public speaking appearances, talking about safety and my recovery. I did some singing. There was a lot going on, and I was out of town almost as much as I was in Bismarck.

This contributed to the lack of awareness about what was happening to me. Even though I tried to schedule engagements around my classes, it was hard to concentrate on learning. If I was speaking out of town, the travel was exhausting.

I felt obligated to accept the invitations to tell my story, and to advocate for health and safety programs to prevent injuries like mine, but I had little energy left over for studying. Most of my classmates and instructors knew I had appointments and speaking engagements, so they weren't surprised when I was absent from class. Except for those closest to me, no one considered that some of the absences were because I was isolating myself in my room.

Darnell was extremely concerned. I started having crying jags. I'd break down, and Darnell would try to get me to tell him what was wrong. I'd push him away and tell him I wasn't going to bother him with my problems, but he was persistent. He'd grab hold of me and keep asking me to tell him what was wrong.

"Come on. Just let it out," he'd say.

"I'm so tired of fighting this," I'd say. "I'm tired of not fitting in. I'm sick of looking the way I look, and I hate being so thin and weak."

Finally, I'd admit that I wanted to die.

Darnell reacted like a lot of people would. He got angry. Keep in mind, Darnell had a lot invested in our friendship. He was willing to do just about anything for me. This was a guy who'd even been willing to help me deal with the intricacies of dating and intimacy with women.

Darnell didn't understand my depression any better than I did. From his perspective, the worst of my ordeal had passed. I had all of life to experience and look forward to. He took it very personally when I said I wanted to die.

"You've got to quit thinking that way," he said. "After everything you've been through, and the way you fought to survive. Damn it, you can't give up. You have to keep fighting. You've already helped people all over the world because you gave them hope. You have to keep going."

"I'm sorry," I said. "But I can't help it. I just want to die."

Even Darnell had his breaking point. After one of those "I want to die" conversations, he'd finally had enough. Out of total frustration, he clocked me one. He was trying to knock some sense into me, and it worked for awhile.

"I want you to say you don't want to die," he said.

"Okay, I don't want to die," I sobbed.

Of course, nothing had really changed about the way I felt. Darnell was not an experienced therapist or psychologist. He was trying desperately to help me, but he just wasn't equipped to deal with my problems. Things were becoming increasingly tense and I had other episodes. I'd say things like, "I'm living in hell." Or, "I think I really died in the accident, and now I'm in hell."

I was on the verge of being delusional. Both Darnell and I were trying to live with my deepening depression, and I know it scared him. The tension kept growing between us. Darnell's approach with everything was to attack it. If we were walking in the Mall, and someone would get in my face, or would stop and stare, he'd get really loud. We called him "the pitbull." But with this black cloud I had hanging over me, Darnell was pretty much powerless. How do you attack depression? He threatened to take me to the hospital, but he knew he couldn't make me go — at least not alive. He'd tell me not to let the things other people said bother me, but everything bothered me. I felt like a freak, and even with friends like Darnell I felt terribly alone.

Toward the end of the semester, Darnell couldn't take any more. Things were so stressful that we were growing to hate one another. Like many people suffering from depression, I wanted to isolate myself even further.

I asked Darnell to move out. Darnell had been closer than a brother. He had endured a lot of personal abuse at the hands of the media. They portrayed him as someone who only wanted to be my friend so he could be part of the "John Thompson Story" and capture some of the attention. I did have a sense that it was unfair to expect him to deal with my emotional problems.

Looking back, it was a painful time for both of us. Like a lot of people with depression, I was filled with anger. I was angry at life. I was angry at Darnell, and I didn't even know why, and I was taking my anger out on my family, too.

After Darnell left, I spent a lot more time with Mitch from down the hall. I'd go down to Mitch's room for a "dose of sanity." He was easy to talk to, and he seemed to understand some of what I was going through. With some people, it was obvious they were only interested in knowing me because I was a celebrity. Mitch knew I was struggling with all the notoriety, and that it wasn't easy for me to meet people that were genuine. He was just a normal, down-to-earth farm boy. Over time, we became close friends even though I tested the limits of that friendship.

Mitch was always interested in how I was doing, or improving. Even today, he can always tell if I'm doing well, or if something is wrong. He says he thought I was struggling to adapt to this lifestyle that I was forced into. He realized it was something I hadn't chosen for myself.

Bob also became one of my closest friends. He watched out for me in the same way Darnell did, but he didn't live with me. I had gone through a couple of bad episodes with Bob when Darnell wasn't around.

At one point, I was so depressed that I was considering suicide by motor vehicle. I grabbed my car keys and was heading towards my car when Bob caught me.

"Where are you going?" he asked.

"I don't know. Anywhere."

"Well, can I come along?" he asked.

"You wouldn't want to go where I'm going."

"I don't think you're going anywhere without me."

"If that's the case, then I guess there's no sense in leaving," I said.

Bob made me give him my car keys. Then we went back to his room to relax.

When these things happened, I felt like I was on a roller coaster that was out of control. I would calm down, and then days or hours later I'd start feeling hopeless again. School had no meaning. Life had no meaning. I believed that if I had to live life as a freak, I had nothing to look forward to. I couldn't see any way out of the pit I was in.

I felt drained. I was hoping the Christmas break would give me a chance to relax, and pull myself together. I went home but the break seemed really short. Over Christmas break, Bob called to tell me he wouldn't be returning for the second semester. Like a lot of freshmen, he just wasn't ready for the academic discipline college studies required. The University told him his grades weren't high enough for him to return the second semester, and they advised him to take a semester off and reapply for admission in the fall.

I was really upset by Bob's news because I had become very dependent on his emotional support. He wasn't afraid to treat me like a normal guy and was one of the few people who could get me to open up and talk about what I was feeling. He'd also roughhouse with me the way guys do. He always said that just because I'd had my arms ripped off didn't mean I couldn't throw a punch.

When I found out Bob wasn't going to be allowed back for the second semester, I called the University and told them I wasn't coming back if he wasn't there. They were good enough to make an exception, but Bob has a lot of pride. He'd decided that he only wanted to come back on his own merits. Instead of returning, he took the semester off to get some experience working as a certified nursing assistant.

With Darnell and Bob gone, I wasn't looking forward to the second semester. But, before I knew it, it was time to head back to Bismarck for classes.

116

Chapter 11
Twists and Turns

Within a few days of returning to the University of Mary after Christmas break, the first anniversary of my accident arrived. It seemed as though an eternity had passed. I could no longer relate to the farm kid who survived the ordeal. Who was he?

The phone rang all day long. There were calls from average people who just wanted to wish me well. There were dozens of reporters who wanted to know what it felt like "one year later." After the thirtieth phone call of the day, I disconnected the phone and locked my dorm room door.

I pulled out my collection of video-taped accounts and newspaper clippings about the accident. It was strange watching this person I had been only one year earlier. I saw a young, naive kid, who wasn't afraid of anything. "He" could overcome any obstacle.

The old headlines read "ARMS GONE, HE MAKES 100-YARD DASH FOR LIFE," "SUPERNATURAL COURAGE," "TOO TOUGH TO DIE," and "THOMPSON INSISTS HE'S NOT A HERO."

"Boy, is that right," I thought. "Whatever it was that kept me going has burned out."

I felt emotionally drained. Looking to the future left me exhausted. A psychiatrist would later diagnose me (in 1995) with major depression and post traumatic stress disorder. I wasn't involved in a counseling or therapy program. It hadn't even occurred to me that counseling or therapy would be appropriate. I figured that was for "crazy people." Instead, I convinced myself I could make things better. I made a conscious decision to change the way I was living. I made myself go out of my dorm, even if it was just to walk down the hall to Bob's or Mitch's rooms. I even went to a couple of parties and had a few dates. I admit, I worked a lot harder at having fun than I did at schoolwork.

I hadn't talked to Darnell since he moved out of our dorm room. One night, we were both at the same party. After each of us had plenty to drink, I approached him. I had wanted to talk to him for some time, but I didn't have the nerve. I walked up to him, and told him I was sorry for the way I acted. I asked him if he could forgive me, and he gave me a big hug. He said he was sorry, too. Even though we were never as close as we'd been before, we were still friends.

I continued to work at my physical recovery. I was being followed by a local plastic and hand surgeon in Bismarck, Dr. Curt Juhala. I was attending occupational therapy sessions three times a week, working with a hand rehabilitation specialist to try to increase function. Unfortunately, I was beginning to experience the early signs of flexion contractures in my fingers. Dr. Van Beek had opted against splinting my fingers after the accident. Initially, they were straight but limp. When they started contracting (or curling inward), we tried splinting them at night, but the contractures progressed quite rapidly. Ultimately, I was fitted with a small hook to increase function.

In addition to ongoing therapy, I was also trying to juggle a steady schedule of public appearances, which involved a lot of out of town travel. I couldn't travel alone, so if my family wasn't available to accompany me I'd enlist one of my friends. Of course, it wasn't easy for them to take time off from school or work either. In the spring of 1993, I was scheduled to appear on the Phil Donahue Show in New York, New York. I called Bob and asked him if he could make the trip with me. He agreed, so the two of us booked our flights to the Big Apple.

It was an exciting experience for two nineteen year-old guys from North Dakota. Ironically, the Donahue show didn't even air in most of North Dakota. The majority of the television stations had pulled it from their schedules because "Donahue was too liberal," by North Dakota standards. An episode in which Phil donned a dress because he was interviewing cross-dressers, created a lot of outrage. This led to the show's cancellation locally. Obviously, it doesn't take a lot to create a controversy in North Dakota.

In addition to the Donahue taping, we met with a freelance writer who took us out to eat with her boyfriend. She just happened to mention that he was in the Mafia. We didn't know whether we should take this seriously or not. We were surprised that anyone would volunteer such information. Given that he had a genuine "Vinny Vinchenzo" look complete with slicked back hair, we gave her the benefit of the doubt and tried not to ask for too many details.

The writer selected the restaurant, which was very trendy. Bob and I were a couple of country bumpkins, so we probably looked completely out of place, but we'll never forget the experience. The waiters made sure we had bottomless glasses of beer and they continuously reloaded our plates with food as our host and her boyfriend told us amazing (though not necessarily credible) stories of New York City life. But who were we to judge whether the stories were factual? We were a long way from North Dakota. When we returned to the tranquility of the University of Mary, the whole experience seemed even more surreal.

By the end of my first year at college my outlook was more positive. My grade point average was horrible, but I felt I had learned a lot about life. I'd made some friends including Bob and Mitch. Darnell and I were on speaking terms again. I felt my coping skills were improving. The public speaking engagements, though exhausting, were becoming a part of my routine. I saw this as a possible career path.

I was preparing to spend my second summer at Courage Center doing more rehabilitation work. Instead of living at the center, I made arrangements to share an apartment in Plymouth, a suburb of Minneapolis. I stayed with the brother of my North Memorial nurse Lori. Jim wasn't home much, so I basically had the place to myself. From a rehabilitation standpoint, it was good because it forced me to be more independent. I had to get my own meals and make sure I got to my appointments.

It was a great summer, but it was over too quickly. August of 1993 arrived and it was time to go back to Bismarck and resume classes at the University of Mary. I was looking forward to seeing Mitch and

Bob. However, If I'd known what was waiting for me at school, I wouldn't have bothered to return to college that fall. I was there for one week when the head of the music department confronted me about my public speaking schedule.

Apparently, several faculty members held a conference about my attendance and my speaking engagements. They decided the school did not want me to speak or sing in public as long as I was a student there.

If they had based their rationale solely on my academic performance, it would have made sense to me. I wouldn't have agreed with it, but I would have understood it. Instead, they told me that when I accepted public speaking or singing engagements, or when I appeared on television, I was a representative of the university.

The head of the music department informed me that until I graduated and had my degree, I would have to discontinue all public appearances. In the opinion of the faculty and administration, I was not sufficiently educated to be a representative of the school in public situations. In other words, I was making the school look bad because I wasn't good enough to sing or speak in public. Since I was a music major, I could see they might have a point about my singing – but I failed to see any connection between my speaking appearances and the school.

My response wasn't exactly what my instructors anticipated. While I felt most of the instructors were good people, I felt there were too many pompous, sanctimonious, self-interested people in charge. My college experience so far had not been a particularly happy or productive time. I couldn't help thinking about the rumors that had circulated around campus and it made me angry that I had been the subject of a faculty decision without anyone asking my opinion. Besides, I never took ultimatums well. I had no problem sharing my opinion with those concerned. In short, I said "I can live without you, and you can live without me. I quit." Admittedly, I didn't express myself diplomatically. In response, the college told me not to come back to the campus — ever.

My parents, family and friends were disappointed, but they accepted my decision. Of course, Beek was furious. Getting me through college had been one of his top goals for me. He kept telling me he hoped I'd come to work for him some day. If I became a polished professional I could give safety presentations, and promote research on limb replantation. He thought we could work together in a mutually beneficial way. Don't get me wrong, I don't feel that Dr. Van Beek was trying to exploit me. What he had in mind was one option I could have pursued. Things just didn't work out that way. I wasn't ready to take on the sort of discipline and commitment college required.

I couldn't see any reason why I shouldn't continue speaking about safety and telling my story. Even if I didn't have a college degree, I felt I had something to say. So, in the fall of 1993 I decided to devote myself full-time to public speaking.

I was not a polished speaker. My style was conversational rather than professional, and I tended to insert colorful language for emphasis. Some people are turned off by that sort of thing, but most of the feedback I received was positive. People told me that I was "very real" and effective.

After leaving the University of Mary I got my own apartment in Bismarck. It was in an older building, and it was in the basement. I could have afforded something fancy. But, I didn't think I needed anything bigger, and I didn't want anything conspicuous. The negative mail I received when I bought my pick-up taught me to be cautious. Some of the locals were keeping track of everything I did, including how I spent my money.

I was living by myself. I didn't have any friends next door like I had when I lived on campus. Since I had been told not to return to the University of Mary campus, I couldn't go out there to see my friends. My apartment was on the opposite end of town, about ten miles away, so my college friends didn't make the trip to see me very often.

I did have a few friends with whom I stayed in touch. Mitch and I would get together once in a while. Bob also kept in touch. They both played football for the University of Mary, so they didn't have a lot of free time, but I could always track them down when I wanted to talk to them. We all went down to Minneapolis as special guests to attend the Vikings versus Red Skins Football game in the fall of 1993. We were really impressed when the Vikings cheerleaders did a special cheer for us. They topped the cheer by coming up to our box to say "hello" in person.

My friend Jennifer had moved into an apartment by this time. She had a roommate who was from a farm southwest of Bismarck. The three of us did a lot of things together, even though they both had boyfriends. The roommate's name was Lori. She was a nursing student and had a natural curiosity about my recovery. She was also easy to talk to. We had a lot in common, especially since we grew up on family farms. Lori and I started to become close, which made her boyfriend jealous.

Eventually, my public speaking schedule expanded. I had agencies trying to sign me. To persuade me, they told me they could schedule me for even more speaking engagements than what I already had. By the spring of 1994 I was averaging two or three engagements per week, and I didn't want to go out any more than that. I moved into a condo, which was a much nicer place to live. I had room for an office. There was a fireplace, and it was much more homey. The problem was, I wasn't home very much.

The more speaking engagements I scheduled, the more requests I received and I was starting to make good money. Compared to other national speakers, my earnings were low, but I didn't want to have my rates so high that I excluded people who might benefit from what I had to say. I talked about the need for farm safety training and the importance of using appropriate protective equipment. I also talked about rural health care and the need for rural emergency services. I was earning a comfortable living, and I had more requests than I had time to do them all.

In the beginning it felt very good for me to talk about my accident and experiences. It was like therapy. But when it became my occupation, I learned it could be very draining. In addition, I still had to contend with people who felt I was some sort of Messiah. And you never knew who the nut in the crowd might be. Some of the sweetest looking little old ladies could be the scariest.

At one health fair I attended, a grandmother-type approached and asked if she could touch my hands. My hands were hypersensitive and it was extremely uncomfortable for me to shake hands or have strangers touch them. I was completely at their mercy, because I never knew how much pressure someone might exert. I politely told the woman, "no."

She wasn't satisfied with this answer and reached for my hands anyway. I was seated on the opposite side of a table from the woman, so I moved my hands to my lap and repeated that I didn't shake hands or allow people to touch me. By now there should have been no mistaking my meaning, but the woman extended her reach. I actually ended up putting my hands between my legs. The woman was undaunted. She reached down, sticking her hands in my crotch and pulling my hands up. She looked at them, then massaged them. Finally, satisfied that she had accomplished her goal, she left.

By 1994, I had established myself on the public speaking circuit. Bookings through "John Thompson Entertainment" continued to grow. Most people thought it was great that I was earning a living through my speaking business. With all the requests I was receiving, I found myself making scheduling decisions based on economics.

If the circumstances were right, such as a request from a worthy organization with a small budget, I might take an engagement for little reimbursement. But then word would spread that I would speak for less than my going rate, and I would be bombarded with requests in that price range. If I explained my rate was higher, or that I was accepting a higher paying engagement instead of a low-paying one, people thought I was mercenary. Some people said, "You shouldn't even be charging. You should do it for free because of everything that was done for you." It was easy to be firm when people took that tack.

I was on the road constantly. Most people thought I was lucky to get to travel all the time, and meet so many influential people. I got to know people in industry, entertainment and politics. One of the highlights was getting to meet first lady Hilary Clinton. I was asked to tell my story when she was leading the discussion on health care reform, and to give ideas on how to improve rural health care, ambulance services and funding. I'll admit, it was exciting to travel and it expanded my perspective a great deal.

I come from a part of the country where 85% of the people are
white, middle class Americans. North Dakota is a very conservative place.
Some North Dakotans are fearful of outsiders, as if they're afraid of being exposed to other values or ways of thinking. It's not uncommon to
hear people say, "I'd never want to go to New York or Los Angeles,
much less live there." I can't understand that thinking. It's like saying,
"We prefer to keep our window on the world closed."

Until you've gone someplace else, it's difficult to understand there
is more than one way of looking at things. But, many North Dakotans
are xenophobic. They don't want people from other states or countries
moving here. It's sad, since one of the state's major challenges in this
century is to stem and reverse the trend of population loss.

Personally, I considered it a privilege to meet people from other
places and I wish more people would visit North Dakota. In spite of the
low population, it's a great place to live. The air and water are clean. The
vast stretches of undeveloped land give you some sense of what it was
like for the pioneers. Actually, most of the people are friendly and there
is still a strong sense of community and concern for others. It reminds
you that bigger is not always better.

After my accident, I met or corresponded with people all over the
world, and from nearly every ethnic group in the United States. It made
me aware there is so much going on outside of the Midwest. I was lucky
to be able to experience more of the world and to become acquainted
with so many different people. I doubt I would have had the opportunity
had I not had the accident. But there was a downside to traveling. It
meant I didn't have a lot of time to enjoy my earnings. I also had little
time to work on personal relationships.

In the two years since I first left North Memorial, I had done at
least 100 interviews with various media. I'd been featured in all the major human-interest magazines in this country and a few from other countries. I had been a guest on numerous local talk shows around the country. I'd also been on nearly every major network or syndicated talk show
and news program including *Good Morning America, Inside Edition,*

Oprah, Current Affair, Jenny Jones, Sally Jessie Raphael, Lisa, Dateline and *Donahue*. *Rescue 911* contacted me about doing a segment, but they wanted me to sign over the rights to my story. We couldn't come to an agreement. Since we didn't actually have 911 emergency service they eventually declined to do my story saying it didn't fit their show requirements.

The talk show circuit was an interesting experience in itself. It was very exciting and alluring to meet celebrities. I enjoyed traveling to major metropolitan areas like New York or Los Angeles, and at first I enjoyed the attention. It was such a novel experience. But there is something to be said about the "celebrity ego." Talk show personalities ranged from the warm and hospitable, to the arrogant and offensive.

My mother accompanied me to New York on one of my talk show junkets. She says she'll never go back. Some of the hosts are just regular people, very genuine and concerned. Others are so caught up in their own importance that they treat their guests like "things" who are only there to help the host advance his or her career, and increase program ratings. I'd name names, but I don't want to get sued. On the other hand, I probably shouldn't be too critical. I was close enough to being a celebrity to understand that it takes someone special to handle the constant attention. You have to have a lot of self-confidence and self-control, neither of which I possessed at that stage of my life.

The interviews, along with my therapy should have been enough activity, but I felt I had a responsibility to tell people about my experience. I wanted the public to know how dangerous farming was, and how important it was to have good rural hospitals and emergency services. I felt I had an obligation to take that message to government. I also believed I had to prevent injuries like mine from happening — to the point that I started to take it personally when I heard about other people falling victim to accidents like mine.

As it was, my speaking schedule was grueling. I'd fly out of state for two or three days, return home for a few days, pack and then drive to another state for a two-day engagement. My suitcases never got put away in the closet. In addition, there is limited air service out of central

North Dakota. The only direct flights were to Minneapolis, Salt Lake City and Denver. Eventually, that was reduced to Minneapolis and Denver. So, if I flew I could count on a layover or having to catch a connecting flight.

I still had to have someone travel with me on most of my trips. It wasn't practical for me to travel to all of these speaking engagements alone. Hotels and restaurants didn't have the accommodations I needed. It was difficult for my family or friends to take time off to travel with me. We'd considered hiring a personal aide to assist me when I traveled, but it was hard to find someone I could trust, and who could adapt to my sporadic schedule. I basically hired my family or friends to travel with me, but it became increasingly difficult for them to take the time.

My travel schedule also made it difficult to have a personal life. At the end of the 1994 school year, Jenny moved to Fort Collins to work at a retreat camp in the mountains over the summer. Later in the summer, Lori and I were able to take a trip there to visit her. Lori and I were growing close and after that trip, many of our friends thought we would get engaged. I thought seriously about it, but with my schedule I didn't think the timing was good. I was out-of-state three or more days a week, and I didn't feel I could take a step like proposing marriage until things settled down.

By early November, I knew I had to let Lori know how deeply I cared about her. I planned an evening at a nice restaurant to show her exactly how I felt. While I wasn't ready to get engaged, I wanted her to know I was committed to a long-term relationship with her. There were roses and candlelight.

"I want you to know how special you are to me," I said. "I love you, and I want to find a way for us to spend more time together."

"I love you, too," she replied.

I was thrilled. We discussed the possibility of changing my speaking schedule, but no sooner had I made Lori aware of my feelings, than my schedule got even tighter. In fact, I was booked eighteen months in advance, mostly out of state, with only two weekends off between November and Christmas in 1994.

In November, I had a speaking engagement in Rochester, New York. Because I had so little time to spend with Lori, I asked her if she could make the trip with me. We stayed an extra couple of days, taking the time to drive up to Niagara Falls. It was a beautiful time of year. The falls were especially romantic with all of the Christmas displays. It got me thinking again about asking Lori to marry me, but by December my speaking schedule was taking its toll. I was close to exhaustion, though I didn't know it at the time. It wasn't possible for me to accept every speaking invitation, but I still felt I owed it to people to try.

One of the last appearances I had scheduled that year was close to home in Ellendale, North Dakota. Just one day before I got there, a kid was run over by his dad's combine. It hit me really hard. I kept thinking, "If I'd scheduled this a couple of days earlier, maybe that boy would be alive." Of course, I would have felt worse if the boy had died after my presentation.

With Christmas approaching, Lori and I made plans to celebrate our own Christmas together in Bismarck before I headed to my parents' farm on the 23rd of December. I was looking forward to going to the farm and kicking back for a few days. After that, my parents and I had planned a family trip to Seattle, Washington to visit relatives. It seemed like a good chance to relax. I didn't realize how much I needed some stress-free time. While there had been some wonderful highlights, 1994 had been a very hectic year.

Chapter 12
The loss

Traditions are a significant part of our Thompson Family Christmas celebrations. One of the things we've always done is make Christmas ice cream.

On Christmas eve morning we got up early. My brother Mick and I went outside and spent time running around the yard with Tuffy. Then we decided to get the fixings for the ice cream. The number one thing we needed was ice, so Dad and I got in my pickup and drove to the machine shop to find an ice pick. We then drove out to the frozen slough to chop ice. While dad was chopping the ice for the ice cream, I had fun driving the pickup around the slough. It's relatively safe, kind of like motorized sledding.

When we had enough ice we drove back to the house. I went inside and made it to the dining room. I could hear my mother in the bathroom. It sounded like she was crying. I poked my head into the living room to ask my Grandma what was wrong. I could tell Grandma was on the verge of tears, too.

"What's the matter?" I asked.

"I don't know," Grandma said with tears in her eyes.

I walked down the hall and knocked on the bathroom door.

"Can I come in, Mom?" I asked.

"Just a second," my mother answered in a choked voice. Then I could hear her blowing her nose.

She opened the door.

"What's wrong?" I said.

My mother turned to me and as soon as she met my eyes she started sobbing uncontrollably. By now, I knew something serious had happened. I stood there for a little while, giving her time to gain control.

When my mother was finally able to speak, the words were horrible.

"Tuffy is dead," she sobbed.

I was stunned. It was as if I'd lost my wind. My chest was pounding and there was a dreadful pit in my stomach.

"How?" I asked. "Where is he?"

I couldn't believe it, so I asked "How?" again.

I was even more stunned when my mother explained what had happened.

"You accidentally ran over him when you and dad took the pickup down to the machine shop," she said. "Mick found him lying in the driveway."

"I didn't do it," I said in a panic. "We didn't see him anywhere." I started to sob. "I didn't see him anywhere. I couldn't have run him over." Then I lost control. "Not my Tuffy," I cried.

"It was an accident, an awful accident," she said keeping her arms around me.

After it sank in, I calmed down a little. My mother told me Tuffy didn't suffer.

"He died instantly," she said.

Mom explained that Mick had placed Tuffy's body in the box of the pickup that was parked in our garage. I broke away and ran out to the garage and jumped in the pickup. As I sat there petting him and holding him, I could have sworn that he took a breath. Of course everyone told me later it was just the relaxation of his muscles. By now, my dad and Mick had already started digging a grave for him.

"Wake up Tuffy," I kept repeating. "Come on boy, you saved my life. Don't leave me now."

Finally, I surrendered to the realization it was hopeless. All I could do was sob and say, "You saved my life, and I took yours."

My mother came to the garage and told me it was too cold for me to stay there with Tuffy, but I wouldn't leave him. My dad, finished with the grim task of grave digging, came in the garage and lowered the tailgate on the pickup. I watched as dad placed Tuffy's body in a large trash bag. Then we carried him out to the grove of trees on the north side of the house where dad and Mick had dug the grave.

There were other pets buried there, but none had been as special as Tuffy. My dad gently placed Tuffy's body in the grave and began covering him with dirt. We were all crying as dad finished the burial.

Everyone slowly filed back to the house except for me. I sat by the grave for a while. When my parents and brother realized I wasn't following, they stood by the garage and started yelling at me to come to the house. I walked up to them, gave everyone a hug, and started crying again. I felt so empty and hurt that I simply wanted to run away.

I bolted for my pickup and took off down the driveway. My brother tried to get me to stop, but I knew I had to leave. I considered driving all the way to Bismarck to see if I could find Lori, but I didn't think I had the strength to drive it alone. Instead, I drove to a section line and parked the pickup on top of a hill where I could look out over the prairie for miles. Alone, my tears came out in a flood of emotion.

I sat there thinking about when I lost my arms. Tuffy had gotten me through those first awful minutes after I woke up on the ground. I remembered how happy he was when I came home from the hospital. He would nestle his head in my lap as if to say everything was "just fine" in his world. I wondered if anything would ever be "just fine" again.

I composed myself long enough to call a Bismarck radio station on my cell phone. I told the disc jockey I had just lost my dog, who was my best friend. She was very kind and played my request for Eric Clapton's "Tears in Heaven."

When word got out that Tuffy died, a lot of people wanted to send me a new dog. It made me feel better to know people understood what Tuffy meant to me. I had a terrible sense of personal loss, and I was amazed there were so many people who realized he was part of our family. Of course, there were some people who said, "He was just a dog." I knew those people had never been fortunate enough to have a close relationship with a pet.

Chapter 13
The wall crumbles

"Everything happens for a reason."

"It's part of God's plan."

"God only gives you what you can handle."

"There are no accidents."

In times of tragedy or loss, it's hard to find words of comfort. Most people don't know what to say, so they rely on old clichés. I understand the need to try to make sense of senseless situations. But I personally find it impossible to accept the notion of a God who micro-manages everything. I think people resort to using clichés and platitudes because it scares them to think about how they would handle the same situation, and they're afraid to face the real reasons things happen.

Sometimes the reason bad things happen is because people make crummy choices. Sometimes bad things happen because that's part of living. Life isn't supposed to be smooth.

There are also plenty of times when we choose to ignore the warnings. My dad, like a lot of farmers, had close calls. One time he even got his clothes caught in the combine. It ripped off everything he was wearing from the waist down, except for the waistband of his underwear. We didn't spend a lot of time dwelling on how close he'd come to death or permanent injury. We knew he had been extremely lucky. No one said, "Everything happens for a reason." We all knew the reason it happened. It was because dad wasn't paying attention and he got too close to the machinery. We still laugh at the thought of him standing by the combine with nothing on but his shirt and an inch-wide strip of elastic. That's how we coped with the all too frightening reality that he'd narrowly avoided being mangled.

It was a mistake not to have a protective shield on the power take-off at our farm, but no one could have predicted my accident, much less the outcome. Suggesting that "God" allowed the accident to happen to me because he knew I could "handle it" was ridiculous.

Since my accident, my family and I had focused so much energy on how we were supposed to act that we lost track of what we were actually feeling. I know I did. My story had become so much larger than life, but I felt very insignificant. I was living in the shadow of this thing, with celebrity status, but feeling very unsure of who I was. The accident had altered my course in life before I'd had the opportunity to really choose any particular direction. Destiny made the choice, and I would have to learn to live with it.

I had been spared from death, and I hadn't lost my arms. My family and I received numerous letters from people who took this as a sign I would do something spectacular with my life. Many read religious significance into the event. To me, surviving my accident was more a matter of personal choice than religious faith. I had to decide to get off the ground and get help. I also had to take personal responsibility for my recovery, unless I wanted to be an invalid for the rest of my life.

Even so, people kept telling me there was some higher purpose to my accident. No one except my closest friends said, "It's your life and you are free to make choices about how to live it." There were even people who told me they would "do anything" to have my life and my money. Some insinuated I didn't deserve the things I had because I hadn't "worked for them." I'd actually considered giving all my assets away. It would have been for the wrong reasons though. I doubt that would have changed anyone's perception of me.

So much of the public's perception had been created by the media. I was aware their accounts weren't entirely accurate. By now, I had learned to be very careful around them. I had first-hand experience with misquotes, or using half a sentence out of context and editing things to someone else's advantage.

The media were constantly changing the story regarding friends and family. Some of them were victims in this thing, too. I will never forgive them for the way Darnell had been made to look like an opportunist. It was so unfair to cast him as someone who was my friend just so he could share in the spotlight.

There were a lot of reporters who were simply offensive. A reporter from a Los Angeles newspaper showed me just how low some of them could get. He met me in Minneapolis to do an interview. I thought he'd want to know about my rehabilitation and my public speaking career. Instead he wanted to know how I held my "wiener" when I went to the bathroom. It made me angry that this guy would fly out from L.A. for a story, take up my time, and this was the best question he could come up with. Was this really a story? Did the public really care about these intimate details?

Of course, the answer is "yes." The public is obsessed with these sorts of details. I'm surprised no one ever asked me if I can have sex, or how I go about it. The more intimate, the more personal or private, the better the story — and the more papers, magazines (or books) it sells.

I told the reporter it was none of his business and ended the interview. Then I called Jay to say I'd never do another interview for that particular paper.

Even though I had been working hard to establish my independence, a career, and relationships, there was so much in my life that was out of my control. Tuffy's death triggered a sense that my best efforts would never be good enough. I felt completely vulnerable and lost. All the questions I had about who or what I was supposed to be, came to a head that Christmas.

Perhaps my parents sensed how distraught I was. They were getting ready to leave on our Seattle trip, which had actually been my idea. After Tuffy's death, I no longer wanted to go. I didn't want to drive half way across the country. I didn't feel like socializing, and I didn't feel like making the effort to be good company around relatives I rarely saw. I think my parents were afraid of what might happen if they left me behind, so they were relieved when I decided to go.

We left for Seattle on December 27th. I don't recall a lot about the trip. I slept a lot. When I was awake, I kept replaying the day Tuffy died in my mind. Lori flew out to Seattle on New Year's Eve to surprise me, which was nice. On the return to North Dakota, I was so anxious to get back that I insisted we drive straight through from Washington. We got back to Bismarck on January 8th.

I left for Oklahoma City, Oklahoma on the 10th. I was scheduled to speak to the National Future Farmers of America convention on January 11th. Just before I left for Oklahoma, I realized I'd scheduled the trip on the third anniversary of my accident, but there was nothing I could do to change it. It was not a good beginning for 1995.

I flew back from Oklahoma on January 12th, went home, and unpacked. Then I immediately started repacking with fresh clothes for a speaking engagement in Sidney, Montana. I had to drive on this trip, so I began to load my gear into my truck. Suddenly, I was overwhelmed by a feeling of exhaustion.

I went inside to sit down. I tried resting on the couch, but then realized I had to get going if I was going to get on the road at a reasonable hour. I started to get off the couch and my body went limp. I collapsed in a heap on the floor. I didn't know what was happening at I was very scared.

"Is there something seriously physically wrong with me?" I wondered.

Somehow I pulled myself back together, and then drove over to Jennifer and Lori's apartment. Once I arrived there, I had a tough time getting myself out of the truck. I collapsed in a snowbank before I made it to the door of the apartment. Once inside, my legs kept going out from under me. I simply didn't have any strength left. Jennifer and Lori tried to talk me out of going to Montana.

"You're in no shape to drive," Lori said. "You could hurt yourself or somebody else."

"I have to go," I said. "I promised them I'd be there."

I kept thinking of the kid who was killed in Ellendale before Christmas, not comprehending how dangerous it would be for me to drive. It was really stupid, but I went to Sidney anyway. Somehow, I made it home in one piece. I had ignored the warnings, and I had been extremely lucky. I did my show, and turned back for Bismarck. By the time I arrived at my house I was physically depleted. I had a horrible cold, and I felt like crawling into bed and hibernating.

I called Dr. Van Beek.

"You're done," he said in a stern voice. "No more trips. Your body can't take it."

Chapter 14
Things slow down

It was almost like salvation to have a medical reason to slow down. Inside, I felt I had a responsibility to continue talking about what happened to me and being an advocate for farm safety, but I didn't want to get back on the treadmill of three speaking appearances per week. At the same time, I felt a sense of loss at not being able to do the appearances. I felt useless.

It seemed obvious that I couldn't expect to maintain a speaking schedule that was booked two and a half years in advance. I figured I had to start taking things one day at a time, because I really had no way of knowing how I was going to feel from one day to the next.

I tried to make changes. I started canceling some of the speaking dates. I didn't quit immediately like the doctor insisted, but by April I had curtailed my trips to one per month. I had been very moody before, but now I was a complete emotional yo-yo. I was already on a combination of medications for anxiety and depression, and they didn't seem to be helping. I couldn't control the emotional swings. I would suffer from terrible anxiety. It would start out as a gnawing feeling and progress to an overwhelming sense of dread, as though my life was on some irrevocable course with disaster. Then there was the terrible sense of loneliness.

I couldn't see myself ever having "normal" relationships with friends, family or with my girlfriend. My relationship with Lori was lopsided. I didn't have the emotional strength to meet any of her needs. We were degenerating into a caregiver/patient situation. Lori was gritting her teeth, determined not to abandon me in my "hour of need." Even though I felt terribly alone, I wanted to separate from people further. The more I tried to isolate myself, the more Lori tried to take control and "help me." It was desperately codependent and the friction between us kept intensifying.

In the spring of 1995, I was scheduled to fly to New York for *People Magazine's* big gala of top feature stories. It was supposed to be fun, and I would have gotten to see my photographer friend Taro again. My parents were going to make the trip, too. It was one of the few things I had been looking forward to that spring. I didn't want to disappoint anyone, but the night before we were supposed to leave I canceled the trip.

Outwardly, I was going through changes, as well. Before, I had always taken great pains to maintain my appearance. I believed that if I looked good, I felt better and had more confidence. Now, I let my hair and beard grow long. It was part of the artificial wall I was trying to build around myself. Mitch said I resembled a wild man or a hermit. My behavior was just as wild. If I did things, I went for broke. I'd stay up for days, then sleep for days. I lived on nicotine and Mountain Dew. I drove to break old speed records. At first, my behavior didn't attract a lot of attention from friends and family because they'd grown used to my extremes.

I had a party at my condo one night and made the mistake of drinking while taking my anti-anxiety and antidepressant medication. I had done this before without any major consequences. This time, however, I had a severe reaction. It started slowly. I had gone into the bathroom to brush my hair, and I started to feel anxious and angry. When I came out, I sat down on the sofa and tried to relax, but the anxiety kept intensifying and I was very cranky.

I thought I might feel better if I went outside and tried to walk the feeling off. Eventually, I decided to rest for a while on the steps of a public building a short distance from my condo.

My friends were concerned that I hadn't returned, so one of them came out to see what I was doing. When she asked why I was sitting outside, I told her it was nobody's business and chased her away. She went back to my place to get Lori.

At this point, Lori was the last person I wanted to see. I wanted space, and I knew she couldn't give it to me. She would want to take care of me. I walked to the parking lot of a video store about a block away, but Lori came after me. Then I got extremely angry. I didn't know I could feel such blind rage.

"Stay away," I said menacingly.

"I just want to help."

"I mean it — stay back."

Lori kept trying to come closer. I think she wanted to hug me. I slashed at her with my hook, an action that scared and shocked me. It obviously horrified her. I don't know what I would have done if she'd come any closer. It still bothers me to think about it. Lori decided to get reinforcements, so she went back to the condo to get Mitch.

When I saw Mitch I was furious. I raged at him with no effect. It made me even angrier.

"I'm in a really bad mood so leave me alone because I don't want to hurt you."

Mitch just laughed. Then he tackled me and held me down. I started to cry.

"You've got to get a hold of yourself."

"How?" I sobbed.

When Mitch let me get up I was exhausted and ashamed. He helped me back to the house. I started to feel shaky, so he helped me into the bedroom so I could lie down.

"I feel like I'm going to explode," I said. "I just feel like something bad is going to happen.

My friends decided to call my nurse from North Memorial in Minneapolis. They thought talking to her might calm me down. They put me on the phone and I was talking to her when I started shaking uncontrollably. I couldn't even hang onto the receiver. Then I went into what I can only describe as convulsions. I was shaking so bad that I lost physical control of my body. My eyes rolled up in my head. Then I jumped up and was standing on the bed. The next thing that happened was that I collapsed or fell hitting my head. I woke up after the paramedics arrived.

I don't know if Mitch called the ambulance, or if someone else did, but I was very agitated when I awoke and saw the paramedics in my bedroom. Thankfully, Mitch took charge of the situation. He put his hands on my shoulders and told me to take slow deep breaths. As long as I had a connection with him, I got some relief from the anxiety and shaking.

The paramedics ordered Mitch out of the way. I was fine as long as I had contact with him, but as soon as he took his hands off me I started freaking out. The paramedics weren't going to let Mitch ride to the hospital in the ambulance with me. "He has to go," I pleaded. They could see there wasn't any other way I'd go. On the way to the hospital, Mitch played drums on my knees to distract me.

By the time we got to the emergency room, I had a death grip on Mitch. The doctor ordered an admission to the psychiatric unit, but I said I wouldn't go up unless they let Mitch go up with me. Mitch said he'd be glad to just sit with me, but the hospital wouldn't allow it. I refused to go upstairs without him, so the hospital said I would have to go home. I was released.

Mitch recalls how frightened he was by the incident. He didn't think I should go home because he was afraid I might try to kill myself. He stayed with me that night, to keep an eye on me.

I didn't share anything with my family, unless I had to. They didn't realize what a mess I was, and I didn't want them to get involved. Lori and I were still trying to have a relationship, but it wasn't a healthy situation. She came from a very conservative Catholic family. They were great people, but Lori had a very different view of life because she had been so protected. It wasn't surprising that our values didn't mesh. When I started to lose control, she felt she needed to do more to take care of me. To me, it seemed patronizing.

The anxiety I was experiencing was more than I could live with. I felt like I was suffocating no matter what I did. In April, the psychiatrist who had been following me gave me a referral to a social worker for individual counseling.

As much as I disliked the idea of counseling, I knew I needed help coming to terms with the hero label. I had to find some purpose to my life. I still believed I had to live up to the image the public and the media had created — but how? One freak accident had become the defining moment of my life. Was that all there was? I had become a celebrity over night. Now, at the ripe old age of twenty-one, I felt the future slipping away. I was ashamed that I had ever been connected with a so-called act of "heroism." I began to think life might be better if I could just return to the farm and be a farmer, but deep down I knew that wasn't realistic. If my parents couldn't make a living on the farm, I sure couldn't.

"I must be a horrible disappointment to everyone," I thought.

When I wasn't feeling anxious, I experienced debilitating lows. My doctors were trying to treat my symptoms, but the medications didn't seem to help. I had tried the antidepressants Trazodone and Paxil (which is also used for some anxiety disorders), neither of which seemed to work for me. In fact, their side effects including drowsiness and heightened anxiety seemed to be especially pronounced in my case. I usually felt more anxious at night, so I would have a couple of beers every evening to take the edge off. I didn't realize I had established a pattern that was only making things worse. I would experience rebound anxiety after the beers had worn off.

It also didn't help that I always felt exhausted. I would wake up feeling more tired than when I went to sleep. I was experiencing frequent nightmares, and I'd wake up kicking and screaming in my sleep. I dreamed I was caught in some monstrous piece of machinery. Sometimes I would dream about other people being killed or maimed in horrific accidents. I relived Tuffy's accident, only this time I could see myself driving the pickup over him, and I couldn't get the truck to stop.

Lori wanted to move in with me that spring and was applying a lot of pressure. I realized this was a terrible idea and said "no." I figured it wasn't a good idea for us to live together if I was an emotional wreck both day and night. I didn't know the nightmares were partially a side-effect of the medications I was taking. Eventually, my psychiatrist prescribed a tricyclic antidepressant called Desipramine. It seemed to help my depression but intensified my anxiety.

By April, the Desipramine wasn't helping my depression any more. I kept thinking, "I want to die."

Impulsively, I started thinking that it would clear my head and help me relax if I could just go to the ocean. I decided to take a trip to the west coast. I needed someone to go with me, but the only one I felt I could trust was Mitch. Of course, Lori thought it was a horrible plan. The problem was, Mitch was in college and it was just a few weeks before spring semester finals. He also had a job. He wanted me to wait until summer to take the trip.

"I have to go now," I insisted selfishly. "I won't make it to summer."

Fortunately, he was planning to quit his job when school was out. To convince him to accompany me, I told him I'd pay him to go along on the trip, to make up for the lost wages.

It took a lot of persuading, but Mitch agreed to make the trip largely because he was afraid I'd come back in a body bag if I went alone. We headed west with no planned itinerary. I was obsessed with seeing the ocean, so we drove to Washington, and Oregon. Then we traveled down to California.

In some ways, the trip was one of the best things I ever did, even though it was very selfish on my part to drag Mitch into it. It was completely unplanned, and unscheduled. We even chartered a plane so we could fly over the ocean and view the whales schooling off the coast. We visited the caves frequented by sea lions, and we saw people trying to save the seals. The weather was terrible, but Mitch still got in the ocean and tried to outrun the waves.

If I thought people in North Dakota had a hard time dealing with differences, I found out people on the coast weren't much different. Mitch and I went into a bar to get a couple of beers and I ended up getting thrown out. It didn't have anything to do with my behavior. The bartender took one look at the adaptive hook I wear on my right hand and said she wouldn't serve me with that thing I was wearing. I thought the bartender had to be joking. The hook is the size of a buttonhook and straps onto my hand with Velcro. It certainly wasn't threatening, but the bartender kept referring to it as a "meat hook."

I was told I'd have to remove the hook or leave the premises. Since I needed the hook to do things like opening my wallet, I refused to remove it. We left the bar, and drove around for a while. On the way back to the hotel, I decided to stop back at the bar.

"This is a really bad idea," Mitch warned.

"Well who do they think they are?" I said. "I'm not going to hurt anyone."

"I'm not worried about you hurting anyone."

I went back into the bar. Mitch opted to stay in the safety of the parking lot.

"Take yourself and your meat hook out of here," the bartender ordered.

"I don't think you know who you're dealing with," I challenged.

People started laughing. Then I was physically removed from the bar. So, I placed a call to the local advocacy organization for people with disabilities. Last I heard, the lawsuit was still being litigated on behalf of the disabled.

We'd originally planned to take a route from California back to North Dakota by way of the Rocky Mountains, but we learned the drive would have been very difficult. It was early enough in the year that the higher elevations still had a lot of snow, and there would have been single-lane traffic over some of the highways. We decided to drive back to Seattle and then go home through Idaho and Montana. Mitch still had to take his finals and we couldn't risk getting stuck somewhere.

Mitch must have thought, "Why did I agree to take this trip with this crazy person?" I was paranoid and moody. On the way home I was experiencing severe panic attacks. We stopped for gas at a station in Montana. Mitch had taken over driving because I was in no shape to drive. I had been dozing and dreaming vividly. When Mitch stopped, I woke up convinced I'd seen Tuffy. I made Mitch inspect the pickup box and look around the gas station. Tuffy had seemed so alive and real that I wasn't willing to accept it was a dream. The experience was very upsetting and I was already in a fragile emotional state.

Mitch was my safety net. He knew I was on this emotional high wire. He'd also seen me at my worst but still accepted me. I hate to think what might have happened had I gone by myself. At least the trip got me away from Lori for a couple of weeks and helped me gain some perspective on the relationship. In my view, she seemed to thrive on having me be dependent on her, but was very insecure on her own. Actually, I was being unfair to Lori. It was a very bad time for us to be together, and very little of it was her fault.

I think Lori resented it that I spent so much time with other friends and seemed to seek their advice. At least I felt I could trust Bob and Mitch. I think they both realized I'd never really had a chance to live my own life after my accident. They must have seen something worth saving because they put up with a lot. I'm amazed they cared enough about me to put up with my mood swings and anxiety attacks. It's not easy spending time with someone whose life is in constant crisis, but they helped me get through it.

It was only a matter of time before Lori and I went our separate ways. I hadn't planned to break off the relationship, but I was relieved when she told me she was moving to Rochester, Minnesota at the end of the school year to attend a nursing internship at the Mayo Medical Center. I had to break free of the relationship and here was my opportunity. I couldn't clear my head, and I wanted to escape everyone who was telling me how I should run my life.

The summer of 1995 was hell. I had another surgery on my right hand, something I didn't feel emotionally or physically ready for. My weight was way down, and surgeries always took a lot out of me. It was a long recovery process.

Mitch had returned to Harvey to work on his family's farm for the summer, so I didn't have my usual network of support. My relationship with Lori continued to deteriorate. Even though she was in Minnesota, we hadn't made the break yet. I went to visit several times and she kept telling me what she thought I should do with my life. I resented her for it. I told her it would be okay with me if she decided to see other guys.

It was amazing how much Lori changed after she moved. It was the first time in her life that she was on her own. She was truly away from the influence of her parents, and she quickly became more independent. It was a good change for her, but it cemented my opinion that we weren't right for each other.

Several weeks after the move, she called to say a guy had asked her for a date.

"When are you going out?" I asked.

She was trying to make me jealous, but when she didn't get the reaction she'd anticipated, she thought I wanted to start seeing other women. In fact, I thought it would be great if she made new friends. I didn't have the energy to sustain the relationship. It was taking all of my energy just to keep from suffocating.

Mitch returned from Harvey when the summer ended. By now I was on more antidepressant medication as well as Cylert, a central nervous system stimulant usually prescribed for attention deficit hyperactivity disorder. Neither medication seemed to be helping. Even with Mitch back in town, I was starting to feel hopeless.

At this point I felt like no one really cared whether I lived or died, except for Mitch, and possibly Bob. Of course, this wasn't true. There were a lot of people who cared — but I didn't think I was worth caring about. I contemplated killing myself, but I never formed a plan to do so because I knew it would hurt Mitch and Bob too much.

You may be wondering why my family wasn't more involved. They would have been, had I let them. I worked very hard to separate from my family. Part of it was that I wanted to be independent. Part of it was that there was a lot of conflict between my parents and I, and especially between my mother and I.

My mother has always had my interests at heart, but we had serious disagreements about what was best for me. Since my accident, she became overly concerned with the public perception of John Thompson, but had trouble understanding my need for privacy. There were lots of people from all over the United States and Canada who would "drop in" to Hurdsfield to see if I was in town. Mom thought I had an obligation to visit with these uninvited guests. Sometimes she even gave them information about how to contact me in Bismarck.

My mother's goals for my life were exactly the opposite of what I wanted to do. She believed I should use my experience to do "the Lord's" work. It was the last thing I wanted. I'd developed a very low opinion of most of the "church types" with whom I'd had contact after my accident. Most tried to dictate what I should think and believe. Many had been deceitful and greedy. I felt myself rebelling against the whole notion of associating with them, and I was really angry about all the people who felt entitled to a piece of me.

I also couldn't shake the feeling that I was a complete failure. The occasional thoughts of suicide didn't even seem abnormal. I had made a serious attempt to help others, but people were still getting hurt or dying in farm accidents. I also felt like I didn't know who I was anymore. The person who existed before my accident was gone. At the same time, I was going against my nature trying to live up to the hero image. That wasn't who I was. I had been told repeatedly that my survival had given hope to people around the world. In reality, I felt I had nothing to offer. I was living a lie.

I wasn't even sure I was a survivor anymore. It made me very uncomfortable to be around my family, because I knew I couldn't live up to what I imagined they wanted. My doctors had expectations, too. They wanted to learn from my case. So, from a medical perspective, my life was an experiment.

Very few people had been through double limb replantation. No one knew what sort of long-term impact it would have on my physical condition and emotional balance. For one thing, the accident seemed to have permanently altered my metabolism. While I was over six feet tall, it was a constant struggle to keep my weight above 145 pounds. It was little wonder I felt tired and weak all the time. I'm sure this may also have made me more susceptible to idiosyncratic effects from medications.

I had a hard time dealing with all this conflict. Life seemed empty and hopeless. I felt more and more like a lab specimen than a person. My body didn't even feel like my own. The doctors always had some new treatment or technology they wanted to try. I was tired of being a guinea pig. I didn't want doctors to dictate my physiology. I didn't feel integrated as a human being because there was a separation between my mind and my body.

September of 1995 was a nightmare. I was having difficulty sleeping and eating. At about two o'clock one morning I started hyperventilating. It was an awful feeling because I didn't know what was happening. In a panic I called Bob.

He and his girlfriend lived a short distance from my house so he came right over. I told him I felt like I was dying, and he suggested taking me to the hospital. I agreed to go because I was too scared not to. The anxiety was overwhelming. Again, I went home after a brief stay in the emergency room.

I made another trip to the emergency room later in September. It started with a car wreck. I wasn't hurt, but my car was banged up really bad — and it was my own fault because I had been driving too fast. I found my way to a nearby truck stop on the west side of Bismarck and called Mitch to come get me. On the way home I started shaking and was unable to carry on a coherent conversation.

Mitch drove me to the hospital and the staff said they would admit me to the psychiatric unit. This time I wanted Mitch to sign me in so I couldn't leave. He wouldn't do it, so I had to sign myself in. Fortunately, Mitch took the initiative to call my parents. By the next morning I wanted out. The psychiatrist didn't want me to leave, and was threatening to file the paperwork for an involuntary commitment. He also tried to coerce me into staying by telling me my parents would petition the court to have me involuntarily committed if I didn't stay.

My parents arrived and the argument ended. After Mitch called them and explained what was happening with me, they decided they had to get involved whether I wanted them there or not. They were very supportive. They didn't want me hospitalized either. I was allowed to have them take me home.

My parents and I talked about some of what was going on in my life, but I minimized how serious it was. I didn't know how to describe what I was feeling, and I didn't want them to worry. There was no specific problem that I could describe for them. Instead, I suffered from a vague sense of doom.

I didn't believe my parents, or anyone else, could understand the unending anxiety and the hopelessness I felt. In fact, when I tried to tell people what I felt, most would ask, "Why do you feel that way?" Some of them would revert to saying the words that made me cringe: "I think there's a reason you survived and that you're still here. God has a plan for you." I was sure this would be my parents' reaction as well.

I was beginning to wonder if this was going to become the routine of my life. I'd seen enough to know about the unfortunate folks with chronic mental illness. Would I cycle through the mental health system with repeated hospitalizations, perhaps a halfway house stay, interrupted by brief intervals where I'd try to function independently? Life was becoming really scary, and that only fed my anxiety more.

During this last overnight on the psychiatric unit, I came to the conclusion the medications weren't helping. As I contemplated how out of control my life was, I realized I had to discontinue the prescriptions.

It was also easy to see that I needed some sort of professional support. I began seeing a counselor on a regular basis. Once that step was taken, I felt I was at least trying to do something about the problems I was experiencing. I consulted my counselor and was told it would probably take six months to a year to get weaned off the medications. I was smart enough to know I couldn't quit cold turkey, but six months wasn't the time frame I had in mind. Within six weeks, I managed to get off everything.

After several months in therapy a sort of pattern emerged. I would do well for a few weeks, then I'd have another episode of acute anxiety. I couldn't shake the feeling that my life was surreal, and I didn't belong where I was. I'm sure part of it was due to discontinuing the medications.

In fact, my life really was surreal. I hadn't yet grasped how the accident had altered the life I was supposed to have. I never played the "What If?" game. I convinced myself that if I allowed myself the luxury of considering what might have been, I might start dwelling on it to the point of obsession. I had tried to accept the way things were because I couldn't change what had happened, but it was undeniable that my life would have been very different.

I was no longer just a farm kid from Hurdsfield, North Dakota. That guy was gone. I had never mourned the loss. It was like I had gone from the end of puberty straight into a mid-life crisis. The result was that I withdrew from everyone.

There was also a price to be paid for my retreat from the public eye. Rumors circulated that I was a real asshole and jerk (and maybe I was). There was a particularly malicious story that I had gotten my girl-friend pregnant and had forced her to have an abortion. Most people seemed to settle for the idea that I was a bum who got a bunch of money, and now spent my days lying around on the couch watching television and drinking beer.

I tried to paint a positive face on things, but as 1995 dragged into 1996 I was still battling for control of my life. In 1996, I bought a house in northeast Bismarck. It was on the edge of town and bordered by a creek. It had a country feel. I could watch pheasants from my deck. I also had a couple of roommates. I thought it would be good to live with people so I wouldn't get too isolated. However, I hadn't counted on the dynam-ics of mixed sex roommates. I had a rule that this was not going to be a cohabitation situation. The roommates didn't feel they could comply, so we parted company.

As I sifted through my emotional chaos, I was still dealing with a lot of physical challenges. I continued to have strength and energy prob-lems. Even when I felt good, I couldn't seem to gain any weight. My clothes hung on my skeletal frame. Stress just made things worse.

I started experiencing stomach problems with abdominal pain and nausea. In November of 1996, Dr. Van Beek referred me to a local gastroenterologist in Bismarck to check for ulcers. They performed a series of tests including an endoscopy to see if they could find a cause for my discomfort. It's an especially unpleasant procedure because they stick a scope down your throat into the esophagus and stomach. As a rule, they don't administer general anesthesia because they want the patient to consciously swallow to help advance the scope.

When the tests in Bismarck proved inconclusive I flew to Minneapolis for more tests. My former nurse Lori and Dr. Van Beek's nurse Sandy, picked my up at the airport. I was a nervous wreck. I didn't know that Dr. Van Beek wanted me to see a counselor at Abbott Northwestern Medical Center and that he already had made a arrangements for me to meet with one.

Lori and Sandy said they had to check on a patient at Abbott Northwestern. I thought that was odd, but I didn't realize it was a ruse. When we got to Abbott Northwestern, they sprung it on me.

"There's a counselor here that has an opening," Lori said.

"But I'm seeing a counselor in Bismarck."

"We know you're still having problems. The counselors here in the Twin Cities are more experienced," Sandy said.

I felt double-teamed.

I wasn't completely convinced, but I agreed it wouldn't hurt to see someone for another opinion. That's how I ended up locked up in the psychiatric unit at Abbott Northwestern. Once I arrived at the counselor's office, I was immediately quizzed about drug problems. I admitted that I had been on some prescription medications (past tense), and that they didn't seem to help. I didn't think I had anything to hide. After all, with the exception of Tylenol I hadn't taken anything that wasn't a prescription drug. I also admitted that I drank occasionally.

The counselor figured I was minimizing my drug and alcohol use. In the course of the interview, I was asked if I wanted to share anything that might be bothering me. I had to think to come up with anything specific, so I mentioned the only thing I could think of.

"A couple of weeks ago I had gone to a park to relax," I began. "I like to be outside, and the park is a good place to clear my head and be alone. I was sitting in my car thinking about what a mess things are, when a police officer told me the park was closed and that I had to leave."

The counselor was taking a lot of notes. I didn't think it was significant until I was told I couldn't leave unless I saw a psychiatrist.

The counselor had recorded in his notes that I was "drinking and taking pills trying to kill myself." That and everything else were basically fiction. He also wrote that I had gone to the park to kill myself but had been prevented from doing that by the policeman. Finally, he said the reason I came to the cities was to kill myself. They decided I had to be detained for my own protection.

I was furious. I threatened to sue. There was no doubt that I was angry. Of course, no matter how justified my anger was, expressing it didn't help my circumstances. I must have scared them because security was called to escort me upstairs to the psychiatric unit. To make matters worse, I wasn't allowed to use the phone even though my parents had no idea what was going on. The hospital also tried to talk me into having all of my admission paperwork filled out under an assumed name. I would have no part of it. By now I was threatening to go to the press. I told the hospital that I was using my own name when I called the reporters.

I kept trying to explain that I had come to Minneapolis because I was having stomach problems. However, I couldn't convince anyone of that. Dr. Van Beek had already left town for the weekend so he couldn't be reached for confirmation. They wouldn't even take Sandy's word on this. Sandy kept telling me to stay calm, but that just had the opposite effect.

Finally, I was allowed to call Jay. He said he'd see what could be done, but he was sure that because it was a Friday night, I'd have to stay until Monday. That, of course, is standard procedure.

This did nothing to help either my anxiety or depression. I was so worked up I couldn't sleep. I didn't have any of my adaptive equipment with me. This made it very complicated to brush my teeth, or even go to the bathroom.

When a psychiatrist finally did come to see me, he was only there for minutes because he got beeped away for some other emergency. When he finally came back two hours later he was very patronizing, and kept asking me about my medical problems. To me, this was a waste of time.

All that information should have been in my medical history. I empha-
sized that a physical ailment was my reason for coming to the Twin Cities. I hadn't come to "kill myself."

I told the psychiatrist they had everything screwed up. "Call my
counselor in Bismarck," I said. "She'll tell you what's been going on."

To his credit, the psychiatrist made the call. My counselor back
in Bismarck told him she didn't think I was a danger to myself. Of course,
she deferred to their judgment, but whatever she said must have given
the psychiatrist a reason to reevaluate my case. They changed their minds
about keeping me and said I could go.

It's humiliating when someone's judgment is imposed on you in
a situation like that. Somewhere inside of me I had enough strength left
to decide I couldn't keep living like this. If I was going to survive I had to
control of my life.

When I got back to Bismarck I received a call from my local
counselor inquiring when I was coming back for another appointment.

"I'm not," I said. "After the experience in Minneapolis, I don't
think I'll be needing you again."

I had lost trust for the mental health system. To make it worse, it
was apparent that the lock-up would never have occurred if I was unin-
sured. Legally they could do it, and they could always stand behind their
"professional judgment" that I was a "risk to myself." Before I was released I also had to sign papers promising I wouldn't sue if I later attempted to kill myself.

I'm not denying that my approach was radical. I know it wouldn't
work for everyone, especially those with severe emotional problems. I
also concede that most people in the mental health profession are kind,
caring individuals. In my case, treating symptoms of anxiety and depression with medication did little to deal with the underlying causes. There
was a lot of anger, and I was still taking it out on myself and those I cared
about. However, I had come to the realization that I had the power to
change. Some people are not so fortunate. That realization was coupled
with the fact that I actually had started to think more clearly (due in part
to the absence of medication). In turn, the mood swings leveled off and

for the first time since my accident, I felt free.

Looking back, I refer to the dark times of 1995 and 1996 as "the time when I was nuts." My family and a lot of friends say, "You weren't nuts. You were just going through a rough time." If that was just a rough time, I hope it doesn't ever get that rough again.

Thankfully, I had a couple of friends I could trust. Sometimes, family members are too close to a situation to see it objectively. They expect you to behave a certain way, and there can be too much conflict when you aren't able to meet their expectations.

It's also very difficult to change a belief system you've been raised with. Before my accident, I had been raised to believe it was important to help others, and to put others first. After my accident, I'd had it drilled into my head that I should be concerned about what other people thought of me. I didn't know how to be what everyone wanted me to be. Sometimes my actions were calculated just to see what kind of reaction I would get from people.

A lot of the things I went through were similar to what other young people experience as they mature into independence. I was trying to individuate from my family, trying to set goals, and find a purpose. My situation was exaggerated because of all the attention I got after my accident. I was under constant scrutiny and I couldn't focus on my own needs. Instead of handling my situation, I was "acting" like I could deal with it, trying to take my cues from what I thought other people expected of me. That obviously hadn't worked very well. Now I had to start listening to my gut.

The problems had grown gradually worse, and it would take time to resolve all of them. But without the medications I could start to determine what was really important in life. I needed to focus on self-healing and nourishing my own spirit.

I also needed the relationship with my family, but I didn't need to live out all of their goals for me. I couldn't live to make others happy. I had to figure out how to live my life for me.

Chapter 15
Riding the wave

As I started to overcome my depression and anxiety, I realized I wasn't angry about my accident or what had happened to my arms. I never got angry that my arms and hands didn't improve more than they had. However, I was angry about the loss of my privacy and the expectations others had placed on me. I felt I wasn't even being allowed to take credit for my own survival.

Some people were critical of me for not publicly acknowledging God's role in saving my life. A number of people tried to tell me I'd had guardian angels who'd saved me and had been looking out for me. It was difficult to politely express that I wasn't interested in supernatural explanations. Many took offense.

A number of people insisted God saved me and I needed to follow God's plan for me. It was fine if they believed that. Unfortunately, most of those people imposed their own interpretation of "God's plan" on me.

I had grown very suspicious of all the people who felt I should be involved in their religious projects. I think faith and religious beliefs are deeply personal. I resented people trying to exploit me in the name of God.

I can understand why some people place such an emphasis on God. There are those who believe in a God who plays a direct role in everything that occurs in our daily lives. I believe our lives are so complicated, and sometimes incomprehensible, that it's easier to accept a supernatural explanation for why things happen.

I happen to think people can do a lot more than they give themselves credit for. We can and should take credit for the good we do. If we start crediting God and angels for all the good that happens, I think we overlook the role we're supposed to play. We have the capacity to do good, and we have the obligation to exercise it.

By the same token, we can be very hard on ourselves. Blaming ourselves, the supernatural, or others is usually counterproductive. I had taken on a distorted sense of duty to the "public" and to the mission of promoting safety. It was difficult for me to accept that I couldn't be what I thought everyone wanted me to be. Life is full of failures, mistakes and shortcomings. We have to work through those problems and take responsibility for our lives.

Since my accident, I also gained awareness that none of us can ever exist as solitary individuals. Everything we do impacts the world and the people around us. Nothing we do is insignificant and no person is insignificant. Whether we do something heroic, make some major discovery, hold a public office, achieve honors, or live a simple and anonymous life, there's a collective purpose to our lives. There's also a great deal of latitude for individual choices.

Our experiences may be unpredictable and unfair at times. My life, for instance, would have been much less complicated had I not become an overnight celebrity. I made serious mistakes, but I learned a great deal, too. I know when everything is going out of control, there are still choices I can make. Sometimes, what we do only affects those in our immediate sphere of influence, such as our friends and family, with minimum consequences. Occasionally, our choices have a broader influence. They can be inspiring or damning, depending on how we handle things.

I wasn't ready for the intensity of the attention I received after my accident. I enjoyed being in the spotlight at first, but the situation got out of control very quickly. It left me feeling exhausted and battered. Writing this book helped me see that I could regain control. At this stage of my life, I'm willing to share my experience to help advance research in limb replantation. I also want people to understand the emotional impact an injury like mine has on an accident victim and that person's family.

I'm grateful for the life I now have, and for those who helped me arrive at this point. My arms were saved. Perhaps more remarkable was the fact that I survived the wave of notoriety and emotional chaos that followed my accident. I've developed a greater appreciation of simple things like the sense of touch. I truly enjoy being able to feel things. I can give someone I care about a hug. I can sense the texture of my clothes. I can stroke my cats and enjoy the feel of their fur.

From time to time, someone will say, "It's too bad they can't do something to fix your hands." Because of the flexion contractures, I have no real movement in my fingers although I am able to grip. When I did the *Donahue Show*, there was even a doctor who said, "If you ever want your arms taken off, I'll let you try my robotic limbs." He did give me a chance to test them. I grabbed my arm with one of the prostheses to see how strong the grasp was and it wouldn't release. It really hurt. Even with their limitations, I'm glad I got to keep my own.

These days, the things that give me the most satisfaction may seem mundane to other people. I can paint my own house. I enjoy working in the yard and doing my own landscaping. I put up my own decorations at Christmas. With prosthetics, I wouldn't have the control to type on the computer. I can two-finger type pretty fast right now.

I can do just about anything anybody else does, except play darts and piano, and that doesn't stop me from picking out a melody on my keyboard. I can certainly do all the things I need to do. There were things I didn't think I'd be able to do, that I've discovered I can do. A couple of years ago I learned I could play pool, something I find fun and relaxing. I've become an expert gardener, another way to blow off steam and it takes me back to my farming roots.

I have come to realize my own lack of expectations was actually an asset. Because I never developed any sense of things I couldn't do physically, I'm constantly discovering the things I can do.

It took me longer to realize I could apply that concept to the direction of my life. Sometimes we expect too much from ourselves and from others. We begin to think we only have value if we live up to all those expectations, and forget that we have intrinsic value. It's natural to make comparisons but I no longer measure myself against what other people expect. I try to remain focused on what I <u>can</u> do, do my best, and leave the possibilities open.

There are so many things over which we have no control. It's easy to lose hope when you can't see options. In my case, no great injustice had taken place. The public scrutiny and some of the rumors about me were irritations rather than serious problems. I just hadn't been prepared to deal with such issues. I could forgive the minority of people who lacked courtesy, empathy and compassion. The physical obstacles could be dealt with, too.

I started to see my life wasn't about the accident. No person's life is about one solitary event, unless we choose to make it that way. I had been operating in survival mode for so long that I'd forgotten about the possibilities of living. If my survival was an inspiration to some people, that was a good thing.

In this world, too many people are forced to expend all their energy making it from day to day. That's why so many related to my accident. It allowed people around the globe to connect for a moment in time, but we all had to move forward.

I had arrived at this point intact — physically, spiritually and mentally. I didn't have to be "that poor farm kid who had his arms ripped off and held a pen in his teeth to dial for help" forever. That guy had gotten me this far and I owed him a debt of gratitude. The rest was up to me.

With a sense of renewed determination, I realized I was up to whatever challenges and adventures were ahead.

Epilogue

John Wayne Thompson has endured more than twenty surgeries since his accident. As a result, his arms function well allowing him to live independently. He is able to lift and carry objects. Although his hands and fingers have limited mobility, he does possess the ability to grasp objects. Minor adaptive equipment affords him increased ease in performing activities of daily living.

In the long-term, John must constantly work to maintain joint mobility and strength in his arms. He will likely have to deal with more extreme symptoms of arthritis as he ages, however today he is relatively pain free.

John, always an animal lover, currently lives with his two cats in a home he is renovating and landscaping himself. He enjoys camping and boating, and continues to sing at events such as weddings and anniversaries. John has also been involved in fund-raising efforts for other young farm accident victims who have suffered traumatic limb amputation.

In 2001, John returned to college to study music and communications at Minot State University in North Dakota.

In the summer of 2001, nearly ten years after John's accident, John's mother purchased new carpet for the family home. Although the blood stains from John's injuries had been thoroughly removed from the old carpet and padding, a vivid reminder of the accident was uncovered when the carpet was removed. The plywood floorboards below were still imbued with rust-colored stains.

John's recommendations for dealing with trauma, injury or catastrophic illness

Be your own medical advocate. You are the expert on what you need. Speak up when a therapy isn't working. Tell doctors, counselors, and family when you want to try something else. Fire those providers who aren't responsive to your needs.

If you are taking prescribed medications that alter mood or are in the first year of recovery, have a family member or friend go to medical appointments with you. It's a good idea to have someone who can help you recall what was discussed. Sometimes a friend is more objective than a family member. Their perspective can be very helpful.

Be your own community advocate. Tell business proprietors and government officials about the importance of accessibility. Many of them are willing to make modifications to doors and restrooms if asked. If no one requests a service, they will assume it isn't needed.

Enlist support to gain independence. A network of friends and family will help you make the transition to independence a lot faster. Don't try to be tough and go it alone. Some people may seek help coping from support groups or church groups. Use whatever means work best for you.

Learn from your experience and move on. This is probably the most important advice I can give. A traumatic injury or illness will change your life, but it doesn't have to control your life. Do what you need to do to get through it, but remember you are the master of your destiny. If your illness means the loss of career or interests, explore new things to do and new reasons for living. It may take time to overcome your loss, but don't give up.

To order additional copies of
HOME IN ONE PIECE
please complete the following.

$16.95 EACH
(plus $3.50 shipping & handling for first book,
add $1.00 for each additional book ordered.

Shipping and Handling costs for larger quantites
available upon request.

Please send me _____ additional books at $16.95 + shipping & handling

Bill my: ❏ VISA   ❏ MasterCard   Expires _____

Card # _____

Signature _____

Daytime Phone Number _____

For credit card orders call 1-888-568-6329
TO ORDER ON-LINE VISIT: www.jmcompanies.com
OR SEND THIS ORDER FORM TO:
McCleery & Sons Publishing
PO Box 248
Gwinner, ND 58040-0248

I am enclosing $_____   ❏ Check ❏ Money Order
Payable in US funds. No cash accepted.

SHIP TO:
Name_____

Mailing Address _____

City _____

State/Zip _____

Orders by check allow longer delivery time.
Money order and credit card orders will be shipped within 48 hours.
This offer is subject to change without notice.

Remembering Louis L'Amour
Reese Hawkins was a close friend of Louis L'Amour, one of the fastest selling writers of all time. Now Hawkins shares this friendship with L'Amour's legion of fans. Sit with Reese in L'Amour's study where characters were born and stories came to life. Travel with Louis and Reese in the 16 photo pages in this memoir. Learn about L'Amour's lifelong quest for knowledge and his philosophy of life.
Written by Reese Hawkins and his daughter Meredith Hawkins Wallin.
(178 pgs.)
$16.95 each in a 5-1/2x8" paperback.

Whispers in the Darkness
In this fast paced, well thought out mystery with a twist of romance, Betty Pearson comes to a slow paced, small town. Little did she know she was following a missing link - what the dilapidated former Beardsley Manor she was drawn to, held for her. With twists and turns, the Manor's secrets are unraveled.
Written by Shirlee Taylor. (88 pgs.)
$14.95 each in a 6x9" paperback.

The Long, Blonde Pigtails with Big Red Bows
Teaching Children Not to Talk to Strangers
The story of three little mice who learn a heart-breaking lesson from a casual encounter with a "stranger" in their neighborhood. This is an integral message that appears throughout the book, to teach and protect our children.
Written by Mary Magill. Illustrated by Barbara Scheibling. (24 pgs.)
$14.95 each in a 8-1/2x8-1/2" paperback.

Charlie's Gold and Other Frontier Tales
Kamron's first collection of short stories gives you adventure tales about men and women of the west, made up of cowboys, Indians, and settlers.
Written by Kent Kamron. (174 pgs.)
$15.95 each in a 6x9" paperback.

A Time For Justice
This second collection of Kamron's short stories takes off where the first volume left off, satisfying the reader's hunger for more tales of the wide prairie.
Written by Kent Kamron. (182 pgs.)
$16.95 each in a 6x9" paperback.

Dr. Val Farmer's
Honey, I Shrunk The Farm
The first volume in a three part series of Rural Stress Survival Guides discusses the following in seven chapters: Farm Economics; Understanding The Farm Crisis; How To Cope With Hard Times; Families Going Through It Together; Dealing With Debt; Going For Help, Helping Others and Transitions Out of Farming.
Written by Val Farmer. (208 pgs.)
$16.95 each in a 6x9" paperback.

Pay Dirt

An absorbing story reveals how a man with the courage to follow his dream found both gold and unexpected adventure and adversity in Interior Alaska, while learning that human nature can be the most unpredictable of all.
Written by Otis Hahn & Alice Vollmar. (168 pgs.)
$15.95 each in a 6x9" paperback.

Pete's New Family

Pete's New Family is a tale for children (ages 4-8) lovingly written to help youngsters understand events of divorce that they are powerless to change.
Written by Brenda Jacobson.
$9.95 each in a 5-1/2x8-1/2" spiral bound book.
(plus $2.50 ea. shipping & handling) (price breaks after qty. of 10)

Bonanza Belle

In 1908, Carrie Amundson left her home to become employed on a bonanza farm. One tragedy after the other befell her and altered her life considerably and she found herself back on the farm.
Written by Elaine Ulness Swenson. (344 pgs.)
$15.95 each in a 6x8-1/4" paperback.

First The Dream

This story spans ninety years of Anna's life. She finds love, loses it, and finds in once again. A secret that Anna has kept is fully revealed at the end of her life.
Written by Elaine Ulness Swenson. (326 pgs.)
$15.95 each in a 6x8-1/4" paperback

Country-fied

Stories with a sense of humor and love for country and small town people who, like the author, grew up country-fied . . . Country-fied people grow up with a unique awareness of their dependence on the land. They live their lives with dignity, hard work, determination and the ability to laugh at themselves.
Written by Elaine Babcock. (184 pgs.)
$14.95 each in a 6x9" paperback.

It Really Happened Here!

Relive the days of farm-to-farm salesmen and hucksters, of ghost ships and locust plagues when you read Ethelyn Pearson's collection of strange but true tales. It captures the spirit of our ancestors in short, easy to read, colorful accounts that will have you yearning for more.
Written by Ethelyn Pearson. (168 pgs.)
$24.95 each in an 8-1/2x11" paperback.

($3.50 ea. shipping & handling)

Prayers For Parker Cookbook

Parker Sebens is a 3 year old boy from Milnor, ND, who lost both of his arms in a tragic farm accident on September 18, 2000. He has undergone many surgeries to reattach his arms, but because his arms were damaged so extensively and the infection so fierce, they were unable to save his hands. Parker will face many more surgeries in his future, plus be fitted for protheses.

This 112 pg. cookbook is a project of the Country Friends Homemakers Club from Parker's community. All profits from the sale of this book will go to the Parker Sebens' Benefit Fund, a fund set up to help with medical-related expenses due to Parker's accident.
$8.00 ea. in a 5-1/4"x8-1'4" spiral bound book. (plus $2.00 ea. shipping & handling)